AWAKENI

PETE GREIG

Awakening Cry

Silver Fish
publishing

First published in Great Britain 1998 by
Silver Fish Publishing, in association with Novio Publishing.

British Library Cataloguing in Publication Data
A record for this book is available from the British Library

ISBN 1 902134 10 9

Printed and bound in Great Britain by
Cox & Wyman, Reading, Berks

Silver Fish Publishing is a division of
Silver Fish Creative Marketing Ltd,
44c Fermoy Road, Maida Vale,
London W9 3NH

To Samie

Awakening Cry is very, very good… It should carry a government health warning!

Gerald Coates, Pioneer

This book has challenged me to the point of discomfort.

David Wilkes, student

One of the best summaries of justice I have read.

Greg Valerio, Cred

Inspiring, prophetic and thoughtful… essential reading for all who still dream dreams and are willing to make the changes necessary to see those dreams come true.

Mike Pilavachi, Soul Survivor

It's always great when someone writes down clearly what you are feeling and thinking. I think that Pete Greig is very cool and so is this book.

Martin Smith, Delirious?

Pete Greig is one of those young leaders that has captured something important about revival in our day. He fuses the dynamic of God's sovereign power and obedient hearts, igniting compassion for the marginalised and lost, through acts of love that dazzle out the pain felt by many. His passion and intensity is a challenge to us all as he strives to live what he writes…

Phil Wall, Salvation Army

If you're trying to make your mind up about revival, and your personal role in it, then this book is fantastically readable and informative — and left us with a lot to think about.

Robbie and Shaz Bronniman, DBA

With passion and clarity, Pete Greig steers clear of hype and revival rhetoric and provides us with a biblical, reachable agenda for revival. Prophetic and provocative — read it.

Jeff Lucas, Vice President Evangelical Alliance UK

Revival is a treasure from the heart of God. Pete does the hard digging and unearths precious nuggets that will stir you and point the way to revival. His treatment of the historical accounts is fantastic.

Kim Unrau, Toronto Airport Christian Fellowship

ACKNOWLEDGEMENTS

Many people have made this book possible and I particularly want to thank the following:

Martin Scott, Jeff Lucas, John Martin, Gerald Coates, Roger and Margaret Ellis, Martin Goldsmith, Greg Valerio and Dave Willetts for their wise comments about the manuscript.

Professor John Hayward, Donald and Moraig MacPhail, Lawrence Singlehurst and Peter Stott for their invaluable contributions at the beginning.

Kim Davies for retyping the manuscript so quickly after its theft, and Naomi Cooke for all her help.

And a final shout to:

Captain Slatts, Aaron-David, Alex, James and Ben, Blakey, Brighty, Ish, Gangster, Kenny, Lisa, Lorraine, Mum and Peter, Tony and Jo, Popes and Kings, Tracey Brannigan, Welly, Wilko, Wolfman and Warehouse.

CONTENTS

INTRODUCTION — THE 'R' WORD

Revival, in and of itself, can be rather a shallow concern. It is possible to clutch at revival as at straws: a sort of spiritual daydream of a time when we will be proved right, our projects will be seen to succeed; a long-awaited, divine "told-you-so" to the doubting Thomases and filthy pagans all around. Such an attitude treats revival as a panacea for all our ills: "Our church may be declining, society may be Godless, our preaching may be appalling, our relationships divided, our witness de-vangelistic and our prayers faithless… but at least we can still hope for revival."

But in contrast to such fatalism, God calls us to address our failures now, regardless of revival. He calls us to bear fruit in season and out of season, to get on and shape society in the cold light of today rather than the hazy twilight of a tomorrow that might never come.

Not everyone is excited about revival; when the word is mentioned to some people they wearily reply "I'll believe it when I see it". Such people may have vibrant relationships with God, but they are fed up with the constant "brinkmanship" wherein certain wings of the church always seem to be "just on the brink" of some new blessing, season or revelation. I am mindful of this as I write this book. In fact I rather hope that people who feel this way find solace in my message of practical preparation rather than blind optimism.

Revival terminology is also in danger of becoming devalued through overuse and misuse. Christian businesses are brazenly tagging the "R-word" onto products to shift units, despite the fact that Scripture hardly uses the term. And passionate preachers can recount the stories of awakening with such extravagant prose that it saps what little faith you had left for your Monday morning reality.

Such froth and misapplication, however, should not be allowed to detract from the reality of revival as an historical fact, a global necessity and a biblical dream. There is undeniably a genuine longing for revival in the hearts of thousands of ordinary Christians who realise that an outpouring of God's Spirit will be branded by brokenness and not triumphalism. Theirs is a hunger and thirst for God to act — not just in the pages of history or in centuries beyond, but here and now, in their families, their workplaces and their world.

Such people find themselves sobered by their own spiritual impotence, saddened by the state of the church and sickened by the sin of the world. They love God's people and grieve that it is increasingly easier to be "Christian" than a follower of Christ. They feel the pain when church leaders fall. They grieve as theologians apologise for miracles and preachers peddle cheap grace, modelling mediocrity and daring to build theologies for it.

And all the while friends and neighbours remain untouched by the gospel, unimpressed by the Saviour, with hearts like stone. Newspapers are full of oppression and injustice with scandal at home and starvation abroad. Television bleeds the pain of the world into our living rooms while we sip tea. But these true revivalists dream that God would breathe upon this generation one last time. This is their prayer, their heart-cry, their obsession. This is an honest heart for revival and I write this book for all those with this blood in their veins, to play a very small part in preparing the way of the Lord.

Preparing the way...

This book is about preparing the way for revival in three vital arenas: the human heart, the church, and in society.

Preparing the human heart

The Spirit of God revives hearts that are prepared and ready; where there is radical holiness, persistent and passionate prayer, faith and an obsession with Jesus. But while radical holiness must always be our starting point it is the contention of this book that we cannot stop there. Personal piety may trigger personal revival and isolated blessing, but our desire is ultimately for something much bigger: a mass-movement of the Spirit which transforms society with the gospel. This means that we will also have to turn our gaze outwards, to face the daunting task of preparing the church and even the world for an awakening.

Preparing the church

The new wine of revival can only really be contained and conveyed by churches that are flexible and willing to embrace change.

Tragically, the church in the west is so compromised and unyielding that our road to revival may well have to pass through the invigorating waters of reform as well as the refiner's purifying fire. We stand in a rich stream of church-planting heroes and prophetic pioneers; from the New Testament Apostles, the Desert Fathers and ancient Celtic saints down through the radical nonconformists within the mainstream and outside. Western Christians must respond to the challenge to pioneer once more. We will have to learn from our family in the developing world: churches meeting anywhere from huge football stadiums in Argentina to secret locations in China. We must dare to apply the principles of Scripture to the tamed and tepid church within which we are so comfortable. We must welcome the winds of change.

Preparing society

Scripture challenges us to transform society from within but tragically we have often done just the opposite, retreating into a religious ghetto. At such a distance we fail to season and illuminate society, and are seen as irrelevant by the rest of the population. We have a mandate to engage culturally, to shape mind-sets, to recover the ground lost to modern ideologies and to reassert the gospel as a viable choice. A cynic once said "Jesus may be the answer, but would someone mind telling me what the question is?" We will have to begin by provoking the questions in a million minds to which the gospel is the answer.

However, preparing society for awakening is far more than just a cunning strategy for friendship-evangelism. Our prayer is not just for a series of individuals to be rescued from society, but that the fabric of society itself might be redeemed. Any gospel which engages hearts and saves souls without transforming society, falls short of the gospel of Jesus displayed in Scripture.

Awakening must, therefore, advance way beyond successful church meetings (desirable as these are) to implement profound social change. Any fire ignited in the heart of the church will spread wherever the tinder is laid. Where, then, will we lay tinder? How far will we venture and how deep will we go in preparing the way of the Lord? When it comes, awakening will either reinforce the Christian ghetto with (wonderful but limited) short-term gains, or it will transform the vast expanse of society, liberating thousands and altering the history books of tomorrow. The challenge is clear: to evacuate the ghetto and advance the Kingdom of Heaven into the uncharted territories of modern society.

As we survey the wilderness of our time Isaiah's awakening cry inspires us to get ourselves and our world ready for Christ's return:

A voice of one calling: "In the desert prepare the way of the Lord; make straight in the wilderness a highway for our God. Every valley shall be raised up, every mountain and hill made low; the rough ground shall become level, the rugged places a plain. And the glory of the Lord will be revealed, and all mankind together will see it. For the mouth of the Lord has spoken." (Isaiah 40:3-5)

We miss you Lord Jesus. Come quickly.

A note on terminology

This book is divided into four sections to make it easier to find the parts that particularly interest you. You will probably want to read from cover to cover to gain the fullest and most balanced understanding of the subject. However, you may prefer to turn straight to the chapters of particular topical interest.

The heart of my message is conveyed in the chapters on preparing the church and society for awakening (sections three and four) and it is this material, in particular, which distinguishes the work from most other revival books. However, the first half of the book lays vital foundations for those approaching the wonders of revival for the first time. It has been a privilege to recount and explore the stories of revival for a new generation of readers.

For 250 years Protestant theologians have agreed on a broad definition of revival as "God's quickening visitation of His people, touching their hearts and deepening His work of grace in their lives."[1] However, there are certain important differences between the popular American and European interpretations of this definition. Since the days of the great evangelist Charles Grandison Finney, American Christians have tended to label any concentrated and successful evangelistic campaign as revival, and in some circles the word "revival" merely describes a context of great Christian excitement.

Whilst appreciating Finney's pragmatism, this book uses the word in its European sense, understanding revival as an extraordinary work of a sovereign God that revitalises the church and transforms society. This view emphasises that revival is beyond human instigation and has a supernatural and social impact way beyond normal Christian contexts.

Is it revival or awakening?

British evangelicals have traditionally drawn a distinction between "revival" which arouses the church and "awakening" which transforms society.[2] This distinction is riddled with problems however, for example:

- How could a truly revived church fail to transform society? As the empowered agent of Christ on earth, a revived church will inevitably take up his mission to the poor and oppressed. If a community of believers claims to be experiencing revival without engaging in the broader works of Jesus beyond the walls of its own meetings, the claim lacks scriptural validity.
- How can we expect to see an "awakening" that will shake the foundations of society without a revival of New Testament power among Christians first? It is our job to outwork God's dream for this broken planet, but to do this we need a lot of help! In fact the sad state of the Western church proves beyond question that she will never again be able to impact society in awakening without first being revived by God. It is biblically true and historically evident that revival always begins with the church before ever it impacts the rest of the world: For it is time for judgment to begin with the family of God (1 Peter 4:17).

Without revival there can be no awakening. With revival there must be awakening. The two terms are fundamentally interchangeable and I will therefore use them interchangeably in this book.

However, I do acknowledge that there may be times when it is helpful to make the chronological differentiation between phase one "revival" which begins in the church, and phase two "awakening" which leaps beyond the walls of a revived church to impact society more broadly. Evan Roberts, in the Welsh awakening of 1904, understood the importance of reviving Christians first in order to awaken society: "My mission is first to the churches. When the churches are aroused to their duty, men of the world will be swept into the kingdom — a whole church on its knees is irresistible."[3]

I: PREPARING THE WAY

Revival is God revealing himself to man in awful holiness and irresistible power. It is such a manifest working of God that human personalities are overshadowed and human programmes abandoned. It is man retiring into the background because God has taken the field… working in extraordinary power on saint and sinner alike.

Arthur Wallis

CHAPTER 1

BACK TO NORMAL

From the standpoint of New Testament Christianity, there is nothing unusual about the revival experience...

Robert Coleman[4]

Andy and I were not happy. We slouched in a large neat graveyard consuming our sandwiches and thinking unusually deep thoughts. It seemed an appropriate place to be discussing our feelings about church; graveyards are, after all, strong, solid, reliable and immaculately laid out, but they are also ancient and rather lacking in life. The school bell would soon sound across the neighbouring playground calling us back for the afternoon.

For both of us, church attendance had begun some nine months before birth, and consequently we had never known a great deal of choice in the matter. Through Sunday School and now youth group we had grown as Christians; wanting to get it right, trying to pray and read the Bible and struggling to live God's way. And that was the very problem we were discussing...

It had become obvious that there was a lot of fun to be had "out there" at friends' parties: getting drunk, messing around with girls and bragging about it all week and we had a nasty suspicion that, far from enjoying "life to the full", we were just plain missing out. Not so many years earlier parties had involved jelly, ice cream and musical statues, which made things undeniably simpler. But now there was an increasing gulf between the familiar world of church and the unexplored universe of girls and cheap cider. It seemed that we were too religious for the parties and too lukewarm for God. With a foot in both camps and this gaping ravine between them, we would shortly be doing the splits. We would have to step one way or the other, to commit our lives entirely to a single extreme.

Deep down we both wanted to live for God. We had meant the simple prayers we had prayed down the years, we knew God could be trusted and we respected our parents' faith. But there just had to be more to Christianity than suits, sincerity and sensible sweaters on Sundays. After all, the New Testament explodes with miracles, arrests, crowds, camaraderie and riotous excitement. Life like that would knock teenage parties right out of the contest.

And so, as we moved on to our yoghurts, Andy and I made rather a big decision: we would give God a go. We had no idea if it was still possible to experience Christianity in the way it had been at the start and, even if it was, we had no idea how to get there from that graveyard, but we agreed to give God a try.

We decided to meet every Wednesday night in a large shed in my back garden with anyone who felt like joining us. We would sing songs, say prayers, break bread, strum tuneless guitars and generally do anything we could think of to try and make God turn up. And God, in his grace, came.

Hordes of thirsty young people flowed through my parents' back garden over the coming year and miracles began to happen. A non-Christian called Mark began to come to the meetings because he fancied one of the girls. He went to college all week and on Saturdays worked in a shop. After work he would invariably go out and blow his entire pay packet on curry and beer, leaving him penniless all week. One Wednesday Mark became increasingly agitated during the worship and eventually ran out of the room. I found him sitting on the step outside.

"Why did you run out?"

"G-God was in there."

"Ah yes" I nodded knowingly, "where two or three are gathered..."

"No Pete, you don't understand." He was white as a sheet, "God was in *there*! If I'd stayed in that room a moment longer," he kept pointing at the door, "I'd have had to give him everything, and I can't do that right now."

The Head Girl wanted to be prayed for. She had heard something somewhere about being "filled with the Holy Spirit" and wanted it to happen to her. People had apparently prayed for her in the past but it hadn't really worked, so she asked if we would have a go. It sounded harmless enough, so my friend Steve and I agreed to try. We started with the obvious bits you have to pray out of politeness while you work out what you really want to say; "Lord, we really just want to thank you, Lord, for your servant Beryl/Mervin/Adolf here and we just pray, God, that you would bless him/her, Lord" etc... After these formalities we simply invited the Holy Spirit to come and do his stuff. Suddenly the Head Girl began shaking violently like someone having a laughing fit whilst being electrocuted on an invisible bouncy castle. All we'd done was pray the usual things and here she was impersonating a washing machine on the spin cycle. After half an hour, having absolutely no idea how to make it all stop, we went and got choc-ices and settled down to watch. Eventually she stopped and said she felt closer to God than ever before. We were deeply relieved.[5]

The awareness of God's presence was so strong in some of those gatherings that we approached Wednesdays with a mixture of excitement and awe. One evening a polite girl with glasses and sensible shoes began to scream and manifest demonically. No-one had ever taught us anything about demons (the nearest thing to deliverance ministry in my church was the annual Christmas card free-postage service). As a result our approach to exorcism owed more in style to *The Omen* than the Bible and, try as we might, we could not make the girl stop twitching and screaming. We were still gathered round her praying nervously when — much to my relief — the door-bell called me away to the front door. But to my horror I was greeted by a sight even more worrying than the demon in my back garden. There before me stood the afflicted girl's mother. I stammered something incoherent, slammed the door in her face and galloped frantically back to the shed.

"Make her stop!" I yelled, bursting through the door, "Now!" But the girl continued to writhe and scream. I ran back to the bewildered mother and lied, "Erm — she's just coming." In the back garden they were trying everything: the sign of the cross, "in the name of Jesus..." Someone probably even gave "abracadabra" a go. Back and forth I dashed like a headless chicken, one moment gaping at the daughter wrestling with a demon in my back garden, and the next endeavouring small-talk with the terrifying Laura Ashley mother on my front step. An apparent eternity later the demon left (probably, I suspect, out of boredom), and a dishevelled but delivered young lady tottered through to her impatient mum.

Those meetings were some of the greatest experiences of God's presence and power I have known to this day and were, I suspect, a small taste of revival. In the midst of our incompetence and presumptuousness God found honest hearts, crying out for his presence, and so he came. We were dissatisfied with the mediocrity that defined so much churchianity, and determined to settle for nothing less than the normal Christianity we discovered in our Bibles. *Then you will call upon me and come and pray to me and I will listen to you. You will seek me and find me when you seek me with all your heart* (Jeremiah 29:11-13).

The discovery of normal Christian experience

The Bible hardly uses the word "revival", and when it does it is in an allegorical sense from which we would be foolish to build a theology. What explanation can there be for this glaring omission? Should we conclude that revival is not nearly as important to God as it is to most Christians?

A more likely explanation is that the New Testament writers did not need to invent revival terminology since their only experience of salvation-life was "revived". Revival phenomena were not seen as anything other than normal Christian experience, and you don't talk of reviving something that is already alert. The first disciples were not sitting around expecting the blessing to dry up, the miracles to cease or the gospel to lose its impact at any moment. There was only one kind of Christianity in their experience and it was dynamic, fast-growing and focused on the return of the Lord. The concept of revival would have made little sense to them in such a context. Only a sleeping body needs revival and, for all its struggles, the early church was certainly not asleep.

Robert Coleman, of the Billy Graham centre at Wheaton College, says a remarkable thing: "From the standpoint of New Testament Christianity, there is nothing unusual about the revival experience... The idea that revival is something of special times and seasons comes from the inconsistent nature of man, not from the will of God".[6] Coleman is suggesting that we should regard revival as the restoration of normal Christian experience rather than the occasional elevation of it. We are, therefore, currently sub-normal!

Most people assume that revivals are only ever meant to be limited seasons of blessing; an occasional energy boost for an otherwise languid church. Some respected revival theologians argue that God only ever intends the church to advance through sporadic growth spurts; loping down the years from one revival to the next — two steps forward, one step back. The history books support this "cyclical view" of revival showing that the church has indeed grown in revival bursts, oscillating between advance and decline. The cyclical argument says that it is unrealistic to expect a revival to continue beyond a few years, partly because people cannot live their lives at such a pitch of intensity but mainly because God does not intend it to be so.

But the early church appears to have lived in a fairly constant state of revival for nearly three centuries! And the history books show that whilst revivals are initiated by the hand of God they are not terminated by God but rather by human sin and Satanic attack for "an awakening might be more like a street fight than a spring morning. A revival movement might be diluted, disfigured, or even invaded by the resisting forces of sin and Satan."[7] Thus revivals come and go because we are in a battle and not because God intends the church to endure seasons of sub-normality. Revival history reflects the ebb and flow of spiritual warfare rather than a succession of preordained seasons of growth and decline. In fact, there has only ever been one preordained season of revival and it began with the resurrection and has hovered over us ever since. Some generations have realised this but many more have missed it. As a result they have not done greater miracles than Jesus (though he said they would) and they have not found the harvest plentiful (though he said it was), and they have not applied his victory to the specific battles of their day.

The first decade of the twentieth century saw the most extensive revival movement of all time touching Europe, North America, Australia, South Africa, Korea, China and Latin America. More than five million people in these nations were saved in the first two years of the decade alone. The mighty Welsh awakening seemed to trigger a domino-effect around the world as stories spread and faith levels soared. The outpouring in Norway, for instance, was described as the greatest movement of the Spirit since the Vikings were evangelised. In India the Christian population grew by seventy per cent between 1905 and 1906, while in Japan the church doubled and in Indonesia it trebled.

Three nations in particular were instrumental in mobilising massive missionary forces: Germany, North America and Britain. It's easy to see the demonic flood behind the World Wars that decimated these nations and halted the global outpouring. Countless people saved in the Welsh valleys bled and died in the French trenches. Who knows what impact the revival decade might have wrought upon the world, had not such evil stemmed its flow? There is every biblical and historical indication that God intends us to live in the ongoing reality of revival, but that the Enemy vehemently contests such ground. How delighted he must be when he can persuade Christians to settle for less than the example of Christ in their lives!

John Stott warns of the danger of relegating revival to the sideshow of an occasional blessing: "Pentecost has been called — and rightly — the first revival…We must be careful, however, not to use this possibility as an excuse to lower our expectations, or to relegate to the category of the exceptional, what God may intend to be the church's normal experience."[8]

In the light of New Testament experience, therefore, the question we must wrestle with is not so much "How can we get revival?" as "Why are we currently sub-normal?" and "What are we to do to change?" And if God revives us, what then? The believer whose greatest longing in life is just revival is like a person whose objective is merely to get out of bed in the morning without ever desiring to go anywhere or achieve anything with their wakefulness. Normal Christianity looks passionately beyond revival to the Reviver and to the prospect of his return.

A love-sick bride

Jesus never expected his bride to be anything other than beautiful, faithful and passionate. His greatest longing, therefore, is not merely to revive the church but to marry her! As we seek God for revival, we are not just requesting another limited season of growth and power that will blaze, flicker and die. Rather we are asking to be restored to full vitality for as long as it takes to prepare for Christ's return. A prayer for revival is therefore ultimately a prayer for the end of the age and the Second Coming. In scouring the New Testament for a theology of revival, there is a great resonance with the ever-present theme of Christ's return. This was the heart-cry of the early church, whose famous prayer was *maranatha*, come quickly Lord Jesus.

It has also been the greater dream of every revivalist through history, to see the Bride and Bridegroom united. This desire for Christ's return is even the longing of creation itself as it groans for God's sons to be revealed (Romans 8).

Understanding revival

We have seen that revival is none other than the restoration of normal Christianity focused on Christ's return. In the light of this we need to find a definition by which we can understand this overused and devalued word. The fact is that revival has popped up in so many different contexts around the world throughout the ages, that it can be hard to distinguish the common thread that holds so many different experiences together. Perhaps the easiest way of defining the word is to find a biblical prototype of classic revival against which we then measure all others.

The experience of the early church

The renowned revival writer Edwin Orr defines awakening as a "movement of the Holy Spirit bringing about a revival of New Testament Christianity in the church of Christ and its related community."[9] This is helpful, but there are problems with using the life of the early church as the prototype for revival, for the simple reason that she was far from perfect. Which dimension of her (highly inconsistent) experience do we wish to see reproduced in revival, and how do we make such distinctions? For instance:

- Was the sharing of possessions (Acts 4:32) cultural to their situation or is it essential in the chemistry of revival?
- What about Paul's apparent restraints upon women, or the disagreements between leaders?
- On what authority do we separate those facets of early Christianity we consider "revived" from the bits we consider flawed?

In practice we accept as desirable those aspects of the early church's life that reflect and express the life of Jesus. He was their (and our) role model for normal Christian experience, behaviour and doctrine. Thus when Peter found himself involved in the apparently "unbiblical" act of dining with uncircumcised gentiles, preaching the gospel to them — and most worrying of all — baptising them, his reference point was Christ. Justifying his actions to the Jerusalem church later, Peter said: *As I began to speak, the Holy Spirit came on them as he had come on us at the beginning. Then I remembered what the Lord had said: "John baptised with water but I baptise with the Holy Spirit"* (Acts 11:15-16).

Similarly, Paul describes Christ as the chief cornerstone of the church. Thus for Paul too, Christ is the prototype for legitimate Christian doctrine, structure and experience; the one whose life models awakening in miniature.

The life of Christ

If Christ is our prototype then the fruit of any God-sent revival will be his works, wonders and words incarnate once more in his body.[10] There will be acts of great compassion (works), remarkable miracles will be performed (wonders), and there will be sound proclamation of the Kingdom (words). If any one of these dimensions of Christ's presence is not evident then we have something less than normative (revived) Christianity.

For instance, if there is powerful preaching with crowds responding to Christ, but there is little community impact and few miracles, we have successful evangelism but we do not have revival. Equally if the church begins to dynamically engage with society, feeding the hungry and challenging injustice, but no-one finds the Bread of Life or the Judge of all the earth, we have something less than awakening.

The job-description of a revived church therefore becomes the messianic mandate of Jesus. The Holy Spirit revives us for exactly the same reason that he anointed Christ:

- to preach good news to the poor
- to proclaim freedom for the prisoners and recovery of sight for the blind
- to release the oppressed
- to proclaim the year of the Lord's favour (Luke 4:18-19).

Drawing these various threads together and using the life of Christ (rather than Pentecost or the early church) as a prototype for authentic revival I have defined it as follows:

> *Revival is a process that restores the church to her normative state: as the agent of Christ on earth. It is initiated by God, in response to prayerful preparation, and it is marked by an extraordinary awareness of God in the community at large, particularly amongst the poor.*[11]

CHAPTER 2

WAKE UP DEAD MAN!

Jesus, Jesus help me
I'm alone in this world and a (messed) up world it is too
Tell me, tell me the story
The one about eternity and the way it's all gonna be
Wake up, Wake up dead man!

U2[12]

Jesus didn't seem to grasp the finality of death. Sometimes he would even tell corpses to wake up! One day an anxious father begged Jesus to come and heal his twelve-year old daughter, but by the time Jesus arrived she had died and the house was filled with mourners. "Stop wailing," Jesus said. "She is not dead but asleep". Sure enough, with their cynical laughter still ringing in his ears, Jesus "woke" the little girl and suggested she had a snack.

On another occasion Jesus caught sight of a funeral procession; the only son of a widow had died and Jesus' "heart went out to her". Strolling up to the coffin Jesus told the son to "get up" and to everyone's amazement the young man did just that.

Paul later picks up the same theme quoting Isaiah: *Wake up O sleeper, rise from the dead and Christ will shine on you* (Ephesians 5:14). Biblically, this is exactly what the word revival means: "to wake up and live".[13]

A matter of life and death

We live in an age of human arrogance and independence. People presume that they are in control of their own destinies, rightful rulers of their own lives, self sufficient and answerable to no-one. In our watertight worlds, fluorescent lit and carefully scripted, it is easy to ignore the harsh reality of our mortality.

I have a lasting image in my mind of visiting the undertakers to see my father's corpse. I had been abroad when he died and felt I needed to see his body in order to come to terms with his death. I was very nervous as the undertaker directed me to the room in which the body lay. But as I forced my gaze onto the corpse in the open coffin I was taken aback to realise that it was not my dad. Please understand — it was his body, but the life, the soul, the spirit of the man had visibly departed. With deep irony, the funeral director had applied some rouge to his cheeks in an attempt — I suppose — to make him look less dead.

Satan will do anything to distract us from the harsh realisation that without the breath of God in our nostrils we are nothing more than dust. He will divert us with incidentals because he fears the power that is unlocked by the knowledge of total dependency. It causes us to pray "Thy will be done", to choose life, to consider eternity, to wrestle with the implications of our sin, to cry out for more of God, to thank him for his faithfulness and marvel at his mercy. In the same way, it is our need of the Spirit that motivates us to cry out for revival; it is a matter of life and death.

Placing furniture

In the nineteenth century a tourist visited the famous Polish rabbi Hafez Hayyim. The traveller was astonished to see that the rabbi's home was only a simple room filled with books and his only furniture was a table and a bench.

"Rabbi, where is your furniture?" asked the tourist.

"Where is yours?" replied Hafez.

"Mine? But I am only a visitor here."

"So am I," said the rabbi.[14]

Those who experience revival seem to acquire a vivid awareness of life's eternal context. It is as though they have glimpsed Paradise and can never again content themselves with the baubles of mortality. Jesus advises us to store up treasure in heaven *where no thief comes near and no moth destroys* (Luke 12:33). James warns his readers not to get too comfortable on earth: *Why, you do not even know what will happen tomorrow. What is your life? You are a mist that appears for a little while and then vanishes* (James 4:14). Another of Jesus' brothers reminds Christians of the eternal horizon: *wait for the mercy of our Lord Jesus Christ to bring you to eternal life* (Jude 21).

Peter missed his best friend and Saviour profoundly (2 Peter 1:14), and Paul even had to wrestle with a desire to depart and be with Christ: *For to me to live is Christ, to die is gain…* (Philippians 1:21). In revival people grow homesick for heaven. Far from feeling stronger, they feel weaker and this causes many to cry out to God for their very lives. And by his Spirit they wake up and live.

CHAPTER 3

ARE WE READY FOR REVIVAL?

God is staging a comeback!

Face Magazine, January 1997

At this moment in time more than a million references to Christian revival, renewal and awakening are chattering their way around the Internet. Everywhere people are expecting God to make a move, anticipating the Next Big Thing. And revival is not just back on the agenda for the church, even secular commentators are predicting an extraordinary increase in faith. Is this merely a symptom of millennial angst, or could it be a sign that God is about to do something big?

The history books make clear that revival is neither a Holy Grail to be dismissed by cynics, nor a miracle-cure for depressed Christians. There have been moments of truth, ever since Pentecost, when God has intervened dramatically in the flow of human history through a revived church. But although revival is a historical reality and a worthy longing, it is not automatic or arbitrary. In fact promises of revival are always conditional upon deliberate human preparation.

Late one night, God appeared to King Solomon to give an awesome promise: *If my people, who are called by my name, will humble themselves and pray and seek my face and turn from their wicked ways, then I will hear from heaven and will forgive their sins and will heal their land* (2 Chronicles 7:14). The promise of revival begins with the word *if*; it is conditional upon obedience. Revival has never been randomly beamed down from heaven upon unsuspecting churches, it attends those who pray and obey. The next great awakening awaits human activity, which is why this is primarily a book about obedience. God appears to be waiting for a church that will prepare the way for his coming.

In 1911 the great race to the South Pole captured the imagination of the world. Most people expected the better equipped British team under the leadership of Captain Scott to beat their Norwegian competitors with ease. But despite having far fewer resources than his British counterpart, Roald Amundsen planted Norway's flag first and returned safely, while Scott's team died a cruel death of scurvy and exposure in the sub-zero wasteland.

The terrible truth emerged that the British team had been totally unprepared for the Arctic extremes that killed them. While the Norwegians had learnt to ski, navigate and drive a dog sled, the British had listened to lectures about polar meteorology and geology. Only one member of the British team could even navigate, their provisions proved scandalously inadequate and their strict regime impossibly exhausting. Amundsen's team, on the other hand, walked a realistic fifteen miles a day for four days, followed by a day off. They had brought sufficient food to prevent scurvy and were prepared psychologically and physically for the ordeal ahead. Both teams gave their all, but the victory had been won months earlier, during the process of vital preparation.

Jesus prepared for thirty years and ministered for three. We, however, tend to train for three years and minister for thirty! Jesus knew the importance of preparation, of sowing the right seed in the right way in order to reap the right harvest. We too must work hard at preparing our churches, our communities and ourselves for the harvest of revival.

The next great awakening

There are many important questions to consider as we make such preparations for the next great season of God's power:

- What impact on society do we actually hope to have?
- How should we cope with a sudden increase in public influence?

- How are we to train sufficient new leaders and disciple numerous converts?
- How will we tackle the major ethical issues of our day if Christians become the dominant spiritual power in the land?
- What will we do if God blesses those we regard as doctrinally unsound (as he probably will)?
- Do we really want "more of the same" in terms of church or is our heart-cry for change as well as numerical growth?

Some people argue that it is ridiculous to talk about "shaping" revival. They say that God will simply bless what he believes in, leaving unbiblical churches or unrighteous individuals out in the cold. But a cursory glance at the history of revivals shows that nothing could be further from the truth. In revival God appears to bless with disturbing indiscriminacy, as Jesus puts it: *He causes his sun to rise on the evil and the good, and sends rain on the righteous and the unrighteous* (Matthew 5:45).

One writer points out that it is a grave mistake to assume that the blessing of God necessarily indicates a divine endorsement of every aspect of the revived church's methods, beliefs and practice: "That there is a holiness that precedes and comes through in revival cannot be denied, but I also suspect that the Holy Spirit anoints what is there, and as a result people are anointed, not simply their "godly" aspects. Hence with Peter he has a revelation of the Father and can, all but simultaneously rebuke Jesus."[15]

John White reinforces this theme: "A manifestation of power is not a sign of God's special approval of one's person or of one's theology, nor does it validate one's assessment of a national situation. God is grieved by our party spiritedness and does not bestow power to prove one group right and another wrong."[16]

Revival of the fittest?

There were aspects of the Corinthian church's morality and practice that were outrageous and yet God was blessing them. And wherever you look at revival leaders, from Wesley and Whitefield to Watchman Nee, you see divergent theology and questionable practice woven in with undeniable anointing and wisdom. The very fact that God does not just use Calvinists or Arminians, Charismatic or Reformed and that revival flows through every church tradition demonstrates that he never waits for perfection before he anoints.

The Great Awakening of the early eighteenth century involved three different doctrinal streams: Count Nikolaus von Zinzendorf's pietistic Puritanism, Jonathan Edwards' puritanical Calvinism and John Wesley's Arminianism. Yet all three acknowledged and embraced each other's ministries, despite inevitable tensions. John Wesley was once asked by a sycophantic supporter whether he expected to see George Whitefield in heaven. "No" replied Wesley, much to the satisfaction of the questioner. "No sir, I fear not. Mr. Whitefield will be so near the throne and we at such a distance we shall hardly get a sight of him."

God is gracious and in all our striving (and failing) we should remember that he has never promised "revival of the fittest"; he anoints fallen people and fills imperfect vessels. This is an unspeakable encouragement but also an awesome challenge because it may well be that when revival comes it "overwhelms us in such a way that we are no longer able to influence the way forward positively, and that what we expected to bring great change proves only to have given us more of what we had before."[17]

If this is true, we should perhaps be relieved that prayers for immediate revival have not yet been answered — such is the present state of the church. The willingness of God to bless is not in question, it is the preparedness of the church as a channel for that blessing that we must wonder about. Awakening is God's business, but preparation and application is ours, so any spiritual deficiency does not rest with God but with us!

The genetic code

As I was writing this book, my wife Samie was pregnant. At first I had to take her word for it, because as far as I could see the only firm evidence was that she had gone off coffee! But then we were invited to the local hospital for an ultrasound scan and there, on a small black and white screen, I watched my first child for the very first time. It was awesome to see that tiny blob, with its heart beating fast and strong and to know that Samie and I had created a completely new life.

From its earliest moments every fetus has a genetic code in place that will determine its eventual sex, many of its character traits and even its ultimate hair and eye colour. I would suggest that many of the characteristics of an awakening are similarly conceived, long before birth, during a vital process of preparation.

There is an urgency to such preparation because when revival finally comes it may well be too late to remedy any deficiencies that become apparent. It has been pointed out that the effects of the great Welsh awakening which began in 1904 were wiped out by two world wars. However, many Welsh converts did in fact survive the trenches only to be defeated by another enemy in the intellectual battles with secular humanism and liberalism. Such philosophies had been developing since the Enlightenment championed by Darwin, Freud and Marx and the passionate Welsh converts found themselves theologically unarmed for combat. For all the wonders of those revival years it remains a tragedy that there was insufficient theological and intellectual depth to adequately equip the young church for the future. Here then, once again, we see a deficiency that could only really have been addressed in the years of propagation and prayer that preceded revival.

As we cooperate with God in setting the genetic code of the revival child, we must turn our attention not just to "in-house" issues of theology and church, but also to the particular concerns and questions of our time. Perhaps we dream of an awakening that will leap beyond the pristine walls of our meetings, to address issues of poverty and injustice. But if our churches are not steering such a course in this present, gentle stream, it might well be too late to change course once we find ourselves caught up in the white-water power of God. Rather than solving our problems, revival might actually reinforce and amplify them.

Revival... with all its defects

Every awakening is unique in some respect, reflecting the values of those that prayed it in and ministered in it. For instance, it is possible to see the New Testament churches echoing the different emphases of their founders. Churches planted by Paul probably had a very different flavour to those established by Peter or John. Even within a single outpouring such as Britain's Great Awakening there were fundamental differences between its two key leaders. George Whitefield was undoubtedly the greater preacher of the two, but unlike John Wesley he failed to speak out against slavery and neglected to strategise and structure for the future. As a result the impact of Wesley's ministry is felt even today in a way that Whitefield's is not.

Catherine Booth was one of the greatest female reformers of all time and the brains behind the Salvation Army which she founded with her husband William. Learning from Wesley, Finney and other great Christian leaders, she combined strategy and organisation with prayer and evangelism. In fact, while William ministered to the poor in the East End of London she would often deploy herself to raise funds from the wealthy in the West End. It was undoubtedly Catherine's strategic brilliance that laid the foundations for the global influence exercised by the Salvation Army today.

So it is essential that we lay foundations today for what God will build tomorrow. And yet, no matter how diligently we prepare, we would be foolish to expect (or even require) perfection before revival comes. In fact revival will bring a great deal of mess! John Wesley once got fed up with waiting for perfection and, during a lull in the Great Awakening that shook eighteenth century Britain, he prayed: "Oh Lord, send us the old revival, without the defects; but if this cannot be, send it with all its defects. We must have revival!"

In December 1938 a German scientist named Otto Hahn was probably the first to succeed in splitting the atom. But he could never have imagined the ultimate potential of his discoveries. Today we know that nuclear power can heal a cancer victim, bake a potato or destroy the earth, according to how it is used. At the heart of every awakening there is a release of extraordinary power, but what do we want this power to achieve? Where in particular, within the broad purposes of God, do we want to see transformation? With such foundational issues at stake it is no wonder that there are nearly two hundred biblical references to preparation. The awesome truth is that God has dared to entrust normal people like us with the keys to revival. In the light of this, Isaiah's awakening cry resonates with fresh urgency: *Prepare the way for the Lord* (Isaiah 40:3).

CHAPTER 4
SIGNS OF REVIVAL

There are three particular features, common to every revival, which are sure indications that something extraordinary is beginning:

- An extraordinary awareness of God's presence
- A heightened sensitivity to sin
- Fervent prayer

An awareness of the presence of God

In 1745 there was an awakening on a Native American reservation, led by a brave young missionary named David Brainerd. He described the sense of God's presence at the moment it all began: "The power of God seemed to descend upon the assembly like a rushing wind and with an astonishing energy bore down on all before it. I stood amazed..."[18]

In the Korean revival at the start of the twentieth century, an eyewitness of one of the first meetings described a similar experience: "The room was full of God's presence... a feeling of God's nearness impossible to describe... The whole audience began to pray... Man after man would arise, confess his sin, break down and weep... My last glimpse of the audience is photographed indelibly on my brain. Some threw themselves full length on the floor, hundreds stood with arms outstretched towards heaven. Every man forgot each other. Each was face to face with God."[19]

This "God-consciousness" generally extends beyond the church walls to be felt by the community at large. In the 1858 American

Revival it is said that as ships approached certain ports on the eastern seaboard they "came within a zone of heavenly influence. Ship after ship arrived with the same tale of sudden conviction and conversion" as they neared port.[20] The captain of one approaching vessel had to signal the Harbour Master to "Send a minister", so great was the distress of his passengers. A commercial ship docked, the captain and every member of the crew having been converted in the last 150 miles.

Duncan Campbell, leader of the Hebridean awakening, marks this extraordinary awareness of God as the primary distinguishing feature of revival: "The difference between successful evangelism and revival is this: in evangelism you have the two, the three, the ten, the twenty and possibly the hundred making confession of Jesus Christ. And at the end of the year you are thankful if half of them are standing. But the community remains untouched... But in revival when God the Holy Ghost comes, when the wind of Heaven blows, suddenly the community becomes God conscious. A God realisation takes hold of young, middle-aged and old."[21]

An entire nation was brought to its knees by such an awareness of God's presence in the Welsh Awakening that began in 1904. Everywhere the sense of God's immanence was inescapable; in shops, on factory floors and down the mines, in taverns and music halls, in trains and schools and ordinary homes, God was present. The cloud hung with particularly intensity, of course, over the great revival meetings. Twenty-five years later, one of those present during the revival, looked back and felt utterly incapable of describing adequately the wonder of those days. "It was the universal, inescapable sense of the presence of God... A sense of the Lord's presence was everywhere. It pervaded, nay, it created the spiritual atmosphere. It mattered not where one went, the consciousness of the reality and presence of God followed... The strange result was that wherever people gathered became a place of awe..."[22]

Holiness and confession

Such an awareness of God's presence always intensifies the human sensitivity to sin. When Isaiah saw God his immediate reaction was to cry: *Woe to me! I am ruined! For I am a man of unclean lips and I live among a people of unclean lips and my eyes have seen the King, the Lord Almighty* (Isaiah 6:5). When God begins a revival work in the church it will always be accompanied by a heightened revulsion at the things that offend him and separate us from his tangible presence. In effect, sin loses its cover.

One of the most disturbing stories in the Bible is that of Ananias and Sapphira (Acts 5:1-11). It was soon after Pentecost and the Jerusalem church was radiating God's power with atomic force. Great miracles were occurring, the believers were together constantly, sharing their possessions, caring for the poor and preaching the gospel. A watching city was impressed and scared and amazed all at once and many were being added to their number daily, whilst the authorities looked on helplessly and panicked.

In the midst of such awakening the sensitivity to sin and its consequences must have been acute. Imagine then, this wealthy couple, keen for recognition, daring to be more concerned about human affirmation than that of God. They sold some property, apparently to raise funds for the church, but in their greed held back some of the profit, pretending to give it all. As they laid their donation before Peter, doubtless enjoying the kudos of the moment, God struck them dead.

It amazes me how many Christians have a problem with this passage, attempting to explain it away or water it down. The fact is simple: sin is serious; it carries the death penalty. By the extravagant grace of God you may survive sin daily, for a season at least, but you must not interpret this as ambivalence on the part of a holy God; the cross will not allow it. But in a revival situation the stakes are raised even higher. The heart that can look in the very face of God in such times and still choose to sin, is a soul in the gravest danger. No wonder we are told that *No-one else dared to join them even though they were highly regarded by the people* (Acts 5:13).

In the remarkable ministry of Charles Finney, the American evangelist of the nineteenth century who won more than a million people to Christ, there were at least five occasions on which people who openly opposed him died within a few days and sometimes hours. In his Journals he reports it very matter-of-factly as though he has not quite grasped any connection! Revival is not a game and amidst the power there will be much pain, and a rediscovery of the fear of the Lord.

Prayer

Every major move of God begins in prayer and gives birth to prayer. When the Spirit fell at Pentecost it was upon a group of people *joined together constantly in prayer* (Acts 1:14). The three thousand new Christians then *devoted themselves to… prayer* (Acts 2:42) and the Apostles knew that their God-given job-description was *to give our attention to prayer and the ministry of the word* (Acts 6:4).

On New Year's Eve 1738 a group of about sixty friends gathered to break bread, share testimonies and pray in a room in Fetter Lane, London. Early in the morning, when it was still dark and cold outside, the Spirit of God fell and so began the greatest awakening the British Isles have ever known. John Wesley described the remarkable scene in his journal: "About three in the morning as we were continuing instant in prayer the power of God came mightily upon us insomuch that many cried out for exceeding joy and many fell to the ground. As soon as we were recovered a little from that awe and amazement at the presence of His Majesty, we broke out with one voice, 'We praise Thee O God, we acknowledge Thee to be our Lord.'"[23]

CHAPTER 5

TRANSFORMING SOCIETY

Revival is a community saturated with God. The road and hillside become sacred spots to many when the winds of God blow. Revival is a going of God among his people, and an awareness of God laying hold of the community.

Duncan Campbell[24]

A community saturated with God

The moon hung high in the sky and the wind swept in off the sea. But inside the peat fire sighed and crackled, casting gentle shadows across the room. On this remote Hebridean island miles from the Scottish mainland, two elderly sisters sat by the fire lost in prayer. One of them was 82 and bent double with arthritis, the other was 84 and blind. Their souls were heavy and distressed by the godlessness of their community, and so they poured out their hearts to heaven in their native Gaelic tongue.

God gave one of them a simple vision: in it she could see the parish church building filled with young people. It was a remarkable image because at that time there was not a single Christian teenager in the village. Taking the vision as a promise from God the old ladies sent for the minister first thing in the morning and let him know that "revival is coming". Somewhat bewildered he replied "What do you suggest I do?"

"What should you do?" they gasped. "You should *pray* man! If you will gather your elders and pray at the other end of the village at least two nights per week, we will do the same here from ten at night to three in the morning." And so a remarkable series of prayer meetings began in the village of Barvas on the Isle of Lewis. The year was 1949.

The two little groups persevered for three long months. They must have been troubled by doubt at times; had God really spoken? Perhaps the old lady had imagined her vision. Perhaps she had been over-tired. Perhaps she had eaten too much cheese. And perhaps they were now all just wasting their time on the wishful thinking of a frail old granny. Perhaps. How easy it would have been to give up when there was no instant answer. In fact God's response took a full three months in coming. But there came a night, like every other night, when a young man stood up and read Psalm 24:

Who may ascend the hill of the Lord?
Who may stand in his holy place?
He who has clean hands and a pure heart,
Who does not lift up his soul to an idol
or swear by what is false.
He will receive blessing from the Lord
and vindication from God his Saviour.

Addressing those present he said "Brethren, it seems to me to be just so much humbug to be waiting thus, night after night, month after month, if we ourselves are not right with God. I must ask myself 'Is *my* heart pure? Are *my* hands clean?'" Then turning his eyes to heaven he cried out to God and crumpled to the floor under the power of the Holy Spirit. In that instant an awareness of God's awesome presence exploded into the room. The atmosphere became charged with wonder. No-one dared speak for the Lord of Lords had finally come. Duncan Campbell (the leader of the ensuing awakening who was not yet on the island) later identified that young man's prayer as the catalyst that "let a power loose that shook the Hebrides."

Campbell was called to the island immediately and invited to preach. The first meeting had hardly been publicised and yet when he arrived at 9 p.m., the venue was full. That service went on until four in the morning with the congregation crying out to the Lord for mercy. Some people were woken by God and made their way to the church in the middle of the night. A group of young people left a dance at midnight troubled by their sin and instinctively made their way to the meeting to find peace.

Now this is a point I want to make very clear. In revival non-Christians as well as Christians feel the presence of God, and it is felt in the streets, in the shops, the nightclubs and pubs and houses. God's presence is not isolated to church meetings, nor is it solely experienced by his people. Convicted sinners will often make their way to a meeting because that is where the people are gathering and the gospel is being ministered, but everyone in the locality becomes aware that "God has come to town" and spiritual ambivalence is no longer an option. Full scale revival overshadows an entire community. It is as though the Spirit of God is hovering over a specific geographical area and everyone in that vicinity is living in his awesome shadow.

God-consciousness

Duncan Campbell experienced this God-consciousness upon many of the Hebridean communities between 1949 and 1953. On one night three-quarters of those converted had encountered and dealt with God before they even reached a meeting, so tangible was his presence.

During the Ulster Awakening of 1859 a young boy became so distressed about the state of his soul during school one day that the teacher was forced to send him home. A Christian classmate volunteered to accompany him and, on the way, led his friend to the Lord. The amazing result was that those two boys did what no normal schoolboy would consider doing and returned to school! Back in class the new Christian could not contain his excitement: "Oh I am so happy! I have the Lord Jesus in my heart." This simple statement just devastated the class, and one by one they quietly left the room, went to the playground and knelt in prayer. Heart-rending sobs filled the air and soon the whole school was on its knees. The wailing of these children reached the street outside and as curious people entered the building they too were touched by God until every room in the school was filled with men, women and children crying out to him.

The same phenomenon marked the meetings which triggered the worldwide Pentecostal movement: "a very blood-line seemed to be drawn around Azusa Mission by the Spirit. When men came within two or three blocks of the place they were seized with conviction."[25]

On Father's Day 1995 God answered two years of focused prayer from a church in Pensacola, Florida, and lent his power to an ordinary meeting. Steve Hills stood up to preach and sinners came running to receive Christ. That flow of conversions has continued and at the time of writing more than 110,000 people have given their lives to Jesus. The *New York Times* reported that "what started as a typical temporary revival... has snowballed into what is apparently the largest and longest Pentecostal revival in America in almost a century."

Several friends of mine have visited Pensacola where they were profoundly affected by the intensity of God's presence. One of them told me a story that clearly demonstrates that this is more than just remarkably fruitful evangelism in that the community at large is being touched by the presence of God. One day my friend was walking with his host on the beach when the host caught sight of someone cleaning the public toilets next to the car park. He approached the man and began to explain the gospel. Within ten minutes the cleaner had put down his mop and bucket and was praying a prayer of profound repentance through tears.

In revival the walls of the church come down and ordinary, unsuspecting people encounter Jesus. It is true that God dwells among his people, but the whole earth is his and everything in it and in revival the living God goes walkabout.

This was perhaps most dramatically demonstrated on the day of Pentecost when the Holy Spirit catapulted the believers out onto the streets. This was far bigger than a meeting or an event; God's presence was clearly being earthed way beyond the confines of that upper-room and, as a result, three thousand people were baptised and countless more impacted that day.

Evangelism

All these accounts of widespread God-consciousness and of non Christians being mysteriously drawn to Christ are truly wonderful, but we must never forget that there are also human factors at work in attracting people to Jesus.

Donald MacPhail was a sixteen year old school boy in the village of Arnol in the Hebrides when the revival hit. At school, pupils were talking about "the epidemic" and all the people that were catching it, by which they meant the revival. Donald became fascinated by "afflicted" class-mates who were so happy that they would meet up in lunch hour to share their stories. "They didn't really try to evangelise as such, but if you asked them about it *you were in danger*...!"

So, of course, when the meetings began in Donald's home village of Arnol, he was curious to discover what all the fuss was about. He was also interested to see the preacher. Apparently Duncan Campbell was a dramatic figure who defied the convention of the day by wearing *brown* shoes, and who had once punched the pulpit so hard it broke! Although Donald had been taught the Shorter Catechism and the Bible at school, he seldom bothered thinking about God or going to church.

Donald found himself fascinated, however, by the very first meeting he attended. The preaching was so straight, relevant and direct; occasionally it was truly prophetic. One night God gave Duncan a word of knowledge that a man in the meeting had made a vow to God which he needed to honour. He went on to elaborate: "You were on a ship in a storm which keeled right over and you expected to drown. You promised God your life that night if he would save you, and the ship righted itself. Well tonight God is calling you to keep your promise." One of the villagers responded, shaking his head with amazement!

The pattern in all the meetings was the same: for the first hour they would worship and pray and then at 9 p.m. the minister would introduce Mr. Campbell who would preach for forty-five minutes, closing with a prayer. At 10 p.m. locals would return home for dinner and visitors were welcome at any meal table in the village. This loose programme went on nightly until "breakthrough" came.

Preaching till breakthrough

Breakthrough was the moment when sinners' hearts began, quite spontaneously, to break under the conviction of their sin. God would literally "break through" in such power that even respectable people began crying out for their lives, so you couldn't really mistake it! Sometimes breakthrough took weeks in coming. At no point did

Duncan Campbell give an appeal, but when conviction fell "after-meetings" were convened in neighbouring houses for those wanting to get right with God. These meetings were the most exciting of all, continuing from 11 p.m. to one o'clock in the morning. Campbell would stand in the middle of the house preaching at the top of his booming voice, first into one room, up the stairs and then into another, as people crammed into every space listening and crying out.

In Donald's village the breakthrough came at the end of the second week. The moment that people began crying out to God in the pews, he knew that he didn't want to get left out. He responded that night but went home in turmoil. The following day Donald missed school, wandering the hills tormented by the filth of his sin and the fear of judgment, and that night he again cried out to God without any sense of receiving forgiveness. This turmoil and the sense of sin continued until, on the third night, he finally received a deep certainty of salvation: "I felt different. I felt clean. I knew deep down that I had been saved. And when you knew, you *knew*!"

One of the marks of this remarkable method of evangelism was that having been left to grapple with God for their very lives, certain of sin and damnation, before experiencing salvation, very few converts of the revival ever fell away. In Donald's village, for example, only two people ever backslid "and one of them didn't make a very good job of it!" Anyone who has been involved in any form of conventional evangelism will appreciate how startling these statistics are.

Donald used to love watching normally respectable people shaking violently or even falling to the ground, not in response to external prayer but purely as a result of the power of God's presence in the room. The leaders, however, firmly discouraged all outward manifestations.

Donald's story was clearly forged in a remarkable atmosphere of God's presence. But it is also vital to note that his school friends had an important role to play in "spreading the virus", and that the gospel still had to be preached passionately and tirelessly with great perseverance before the breakthrough came.

Similarly, the Ulster schoolboy who had to be sent home experienced a unique visitation from God, which was a mark of the revival atmosphere of that place at that time. But his friend had still to walk with him and witness to him before the greater work of revival could visit the entire school.

In Pensacola it is extraordinary that a toilet cleaner should repent so readily (as any that endeavour to evangelise in non-revival environments know). But note that the Christian had still to initiate the discussion, explain the gospel and pray with him.

From all of these examples we can see that the evangelistic mandate continues in the midst of revival. In fact, the need for each Christian to "do the work of an evangelist" is actually heightened and intensified by revival. That work will certainly be made wonderfully easier by the immanence of God but it is not replaced or superseded.

Social transformation

We have seen that revival impacts society with a sense of God's closeness and with amazingly successful evangelism. But it also impacts the very fabric of society: the arts, industry, education and politics. In revival salvation comes to society itself, as well as the individuals within it.

We tend, in the West, to exalt the status of the individual over and above the corporate in a way quite alien to the majority of the world, and certainly far from the mind-set of the Gospel writers. As a result we have often perceived revival purely in terms of personal sin and salvation and failed to acknowledge the seriousness of corporate sin, which requires corporate redemption. However, it is clear that historically revival's impact is far more profound than just the sum of a large number of salvations. Social transformation (as well as personal salvation) has branded awakenings from first century Ephesus to those of eighteenth century Britain and twentieth century Wales and Argentina.

Ephesus

It is said of Paul that he brought riot or revival wherever he went. In Ephesus he did both. He had been preaching and reasoning with the citizens for two and a half years amidst some of the most remarkable miracles ever recorded. Crowds were receiving his message gladly and responding radically by publicly confessing sin. Some sorcerers even burned their occult books and idols, valued at hundreds of thousands of pounds by today's standards. Gradually the Kingdom of Heaven began to challenge the very power-base of that city, outraging those vultures who had developed lucrative businesses around its immorality. The showdown that ensued was inevitable: the Lord of all the earth was moving in their city and the worldly authorities and demonic principalities could do nothing but manifest anger and fear. Speaking for that principality Demetrius said: *"There is danger not only that our trade will lose its good name, but also that the temple of the great goddess Artemis will be discredited and the goddess herself, who is worshipped throughout the province of Asia and the world, will be robbed of her divine majesty…" Soon the whole city was in an uproar* (Acts 19:27, 29).

The revival was not only converting large numbers to Christ. It was also having profound economic, political and social implications as the Kingdom of Heaven dismantled structures of sin.

Fifteenth Century Florence

One of the most dramatic examples of the role that revival can play in transforming society is the awakening that came to Florence, Italy between 1496 and 1498.[26] A young Roman Catholic monk named Savonarola began to prophecy to the city about its corruption. Vast crowds gathered in Florence Cathedral to hear his message and sometimes his face would literally shine as he preached. Occasionally he would sit in the pulpit lost in a trance for up to five hours. Savonarola's prophetic gifting had to be taken very seriously indeed, particularly when he accurately predicted the death of the city ruler, the Pope and the King of Naples in a single year. At the start of his public ministry he told the congregation that he would only be with them for eight more years. He also predicted that God would punish Florence with an invasion from across the Alps. Sure enough, King Charles VIII of France led his armies across the mountains to attack Italy. But incredibly, Savonarola went alone to intercept the advancing army and twice succeeded in persuading King Charles to turn back.

The corrupt city government was overthrown and Savonarola instructed the people in establishing a democratic system. The morality of the city was also transformed. Merchants made restitution to the people they had exploited through overcharging. Children marched from house to house singing hymns and calling citizens to repent and empty their houses of every "vanity". An enormous octagonal pyramid was erected in the public square out of pornography, masks, wigs and idols. It towered on seven levels, sixty feet high and had a circumference of two hundred and forty feet. Bells tolled solemnly as the crowds sang hymns watching the flames consume the pyre and purify their city.

Savonarola outraged the corrupt Pope, cardinals and many priests. Years before Luther's reformation he responded to his excommunication by asserting that the Pope was a fallible sinner like everyone else. Although he was a committed Roman Catholic, he accused Pope Alexander of having bought his position and of being an unbeliever. He was severely tortured in an attempt to force him into confessing heresy. First his hands were tied behind his back and the rope held as he was dropped from a great height to dislocate his shoulders. Several times they applied burning coals to his feet but he refused to recant, stumbling back to his cell to pray that God would forgive them. Finally Savonarola was executed before a mob of onlookers and a strange silence descended upon them to hear his last words: "Should I not die willingly for Him who suffered so much for me?" As his body was hung on public display, many realised that his remarkable ministry had indeed lasted exactly eight years.

Eighteenth Century Britain

Prior to the Great Awakening of the eighteenth century, Britain was in a state of political unrest and social instability. Across the channel the French Revolution was imminent and the monarchy was just as vulnerable in Britain. Both societies were riddled with injustice and the poor were terribly oppressed. In fact Britain was probably even more corrupt politically, socially and morally than France, leading a number of respected historians to argue that it was primarily the social transformation brought about by the awakening that averted a bloody uprising and civil war in Britain mirroring the one in France.

Some evangelists took their message outside of the churches to reach the poor, illiterate and unchurched. Understanding the profound social implications of the gospel, these militants set about challenging injustice and providing for the oppressed. Wesley stood out in particular as he began reforming the prisons, establishing food and clothing dispensaries for the poor and developing schools. The first Trade Union and the abolition of slavery find their roots in this revival. Even George Whitefield disrupted local economies because such great numbers left their workplaces to go and hear him.

Welsh Awakening

In the 1904 Welsh awakening the impact on the wider community was also very notable. The police made the astounding comment that "things are easy for us now." For example in Glamorgan drunkenness convictions fell from 10,528 in 1903 to 5,400 in 1905. Mine owners noticed that coal production was slowing down and launched an investigation. The investigators discovered that the coal output was down because the pit-ponies were working less efficiently. This was because the ponies had been trained to obey swear words that the converted miners would no longer use!

Gypsy Revival

In the last ten years more than fifteen thousand gypsies have come to Christ in the UK under the leadership, among others, of a scrap metal dealer called Davey Jones. In some areas this has transformed gypsy culture dramatically. One notorious gypsy encampment near Leatherhead in Surrey was touched by revival and every single inhabitant was saved. Violence decreased as they abandoned alcohol and forged motor documentation was replaced by legal paperwork. Police were bewildered by the change and the local council even invited the gypsies to rename their site as a testimony to the profound transformation Christ had brought. Today you will find *Salvation Place* where once there was crime, alcoholism and deception.

Buenos Aires

Great tracts of Argentina are aflame with awakening even as I write. The largest maximum security prison in Buenos Aires, Olmos, has been transformed by the gospel. Where once the prison had a reputation for violence and the occult, today more than forty per cent of prisoners confess Christ, meeting six days a week to pray. The social impact is marked by the fact that while eighty-four per cent of Argentinean prisoners normally re-offend, only four per cent do so after release from Olmos. A favourite saying among inmates is "Neither my mother, nor electric shock torture, nor beating by the police, could change my life. Only Jesus could do that."[27]

We will look later on at the impact of revival in terms of social justice. For the time being however, it will suffice to say that true revival is far bigger than church meetings in terms of it's scope and impact. Revival brings spiritual sensitivity and righteousness to the very heart of communities and even nations. Normal Christianity will wake the dead and shake the church but it will also shape the society it inhabits.

II: PREPARING THE HEART

When the voice of the Lord has awakened the church, the church will awaken the Lord and the power of God will be manifested in the saving of sinners.

Arthur Wallis

CHAPTER 6

WILDERNESS

Wilderness: the place of preparation

It was an ancient Near Eastern custom to employ road-sweepers who would run ahead of a travelling monarch to clear away the rubbish from the road. John the Baptist adopted this role as Jesus' forerunner, clearing away the sin that obstructs human hearts and communities from receiving the King of Kings. He was the prophetic voice described so many years earlier by Isaiah: *A voice of one calling: "In the desert prepare the way of the Lord; make straight in the wilderness a highway for our God*" (Isaiah 40:3).

For years I misread the punctuation of this passage as, "A voice of one calling in the desert: 'Prepare the way of the Lord.'" The important bit, I thought, was that we should "prepare" and the verse could equally well read "a voice of one calling at the bus stop: 'prepare…'" I considered it irrelevant that the voice happened to be in the desert at the time, but thoughtful of Isaiah to set the scene for us, nonetheless.

However, the passage actually says *In the desert prepare…* In other words, the place of preparation matters, and it is to be the desert. Isaiah isn't just saying "Get ready for the coming King", but rather he is saying, "Go out into the desert and get ready because it is *there* that the King will come." John the Baptist knew that Isaiah's prophesy was like a map indicating that the King would come to the wastelands first. Central to his message, therefore, was the prophetic theme that the dry and arid desert is the appropriate environment for repentance and holiness.

Jesus understood this too, visiting the desert to be baptised by John which then propelled him even further into the wilds to be tempted for over a month. It was this period of rigorous desert warfare that launched Jesus' public ministry.

Jesus was not merely heading off into the desert on an ill-advised camping trip; he was deliberately, and with grim determination, retracing the steps of his forefathers through the wilderness to the promised land. He sensed instinctively that Israel's wilderness years had to be redeemed in order to unlock Jehovah's original purpose for his people. The desert had become the dual symbol of God's guidance and Israel's rebellion and so Jesus went there to seek guidance and to defy rebellion with obedience, submitting to the will and the word of God in the face of fierce temptation.

Jesus' time in the desert also teaches us an important lesson about the road to blessing. It is the teaching of Scripture and the experience of saints down the ages, that the precursor to personal and corporate revival is often an experience of great spiritual dryness. God gives his living water to people who are thirsty and tends not to waste it on those who are content. Perhaps David was in the Judean desert himself when he wrote: *O God, you are my God, earnestly I seek you; my soul thirsts for you, my body longs for you, in a dry and weary land where there is no water* (Psalm 63:1).

The wilderness of the Soul

Even today you can only access Jerusalem via desert. In the same way, you cannot by-pass trials and hardship on your spiritual journey. Consider the following examples:

- Abraham walked into the desert with his only son, laid him down and dared to raise the knife. Imagine his inner turmoil and desperation, the confusion that preceded the blessing of that God-sent ram.
- It was in the desert that Jacob wrestled with God, crying out for his true identity, feeling like a fraud and yet sensing the reality of his call. Despair, confusion, wrestling with God: these things often precede the blessing.

- Joseph's road to blessing was a circuitous route through family breakdown and false imprisonment.
- Moses worked for forty years as a shepherd while on the run.
- Ezekiel lived in exile "by the rivers of Babylon."
- Jeremiah was perpetually rejected and even imprisoned down a well.
- Hosea married a prostitute.
- Daniel passed through the lion's den.
- Jesus walked the desert road to Jerusalem, anticipating Gethsemane and Golgotha long before Paradise.

No wonder Paul links *knowing the power of Christ's resurrection* with *sharing in his sufferings* (Philippians 3:10). Yet how slow we can be to understand the significance of such wilderness experiences in our own lives, often assuming that God only allows pleasant feelings, despite the weight of biblical evidence to the contrary.

The sixteenth century Spanish mystic, St. John of the Cross, described such wilderness experiences as "the dark night of the soul… in this time of dryness, spiritual people undergo great trials… They believe that spiritual blessings are a thing of the past, and that God has abandoned them… The soul undergoes great pain and distress, and on top of all this, because of the feeling of being isolated and abandoned in this dark night, the soul is unable to find any comfort or help from any teacher or spiritual adviser."[28] Perhaps that sounds familiar?

This is not a call for Christian masochism however. We are not supposed to like the desert, or even to pray for it. You don't find any biblical character jumping up and down with excitement at the prospect of deprivation. Self-flagellation, cold showers and horse-hair boxer shorts do *not* precipitate revival!

However, it has been the experience of Jesus' followers for two thousand years that he takes us into the wilderness to test and mature us. This can be a place of emotional austerity, spiritual dryness and even physical deprivation or pain. At such times God may keep silent and our prayers just seem to bounce off the ceiling. We feel like Job who wrote: *I cry out to you, O God, but you do not answer; I stand up, but you merely look at me* (Job 30:20).

At times like these we find out who we are and (suitably humbled) who God is. We find that, in the words of Martin Luther, "Until a man is nothing, God can make nothing out of him."

Hope in the wilderness

However, we also find that the desert is a place of hope, a place of preparation and a place of provision. Even amidst such barrenness ravens might surprise us with food and occasional springs refresh us. In fact it is when you find yourself in a place of spiritual dryness, that you are perfectly positioned to echo John the Baptist's awakening cry: "Get ready!" — for it is in the midst of hardship, loneliness and thirst that God's highway will be constructed. So often people discount themselves from the blessing because they are struggling with discouragement, temptation or doubt. Yet, ironically such trials may well be the very things that actually put them in a position to receive the blessing.

David Brainerd's diary recounts the remarkable story of his mission to the Native Americans of Delaware. Less than a week before the revival began he was on the verge of giving up: "My rising hopes, respecting the conversion of the Indians, have been so often dashed that my spirit is, as it were, broken and courage wasted, and I hardly dare hope." (August 2nd 1745).

Later he describes in greater detail this sense of wilderness prior to the breakthrough: "It is remarkable that God began his work among the Indians at a time when I had the least hope of seeing a work of grace propagated amongst them. I was ready to look upon myself as a burden, and began to entertain serious thoughts about giving up my mission. I do not know that my hopes were ever reduced to so low an ebb. And yet this was the very season that God saw fit to begin this glorious work!"[29]

A hundred years after Brainerd wrote this and on a continent far away from the American reservations, the same principle was still at work. The pioneer missionaries to the Congo experienced the same desolation of spirit prior to remarkable blessing. In fact, they were so discouraged and disappointed that they called a group of about one hundred and twenty people together to say goodbye. They announced that after years of toil with negligible fruit they were giving up and going home to Europe. But at this most unlikely of moments the Holy Spirit broke through. Many began to speak out in languages that were foreign to them. The missionaries listened with amazement to the Africans, unknowingly proclaiming the wonders of God in fluent and flawless French, English, German and other languages. They were even pronouncing sounds that their Luban tongue and dialect are normally unable to utter, such as the *r* sound. God's work multiplied and tens of thousands of people turned to Christ in the months that followed. At the very moment of lowest ebb the tide had turned with colossal power.[30]

The reality of hope in the wilderness is a recurring theme in the Bible. The people of Israel endured the desert for forty years in the hope of reaching "a land flowing with milk and honey." Isaiah foresaw a day when *the Spirit is poured upon us from on high, and the desert becomes a fertile field* (Isaiah 32:15). Taking this literally the Israeli Government established kibbutzes with the vision of cultivating their wilderness until it *bursts into bloom* (Isaiah 35:1). It is a remarkable visual aid today to see vast expanses of green with citrus groves, ripe and fertile where once there was only desert.

Together in the wilderness

The desert is not just a place of personal preparation for personal revival, however. It is often groups, communities or even nations that find themselves in the wastelands crying out to God.

A few years ago our church was developing well, we were growing fast and the future seemed exciting. But then the ground began to get harder, meetings were dryer, leaders began to burn out, prayer meetings were shrinking and the growth slowed down. But out of this dryness we began to cry out to God; it reminded us of how much we need him. As a result the prayer meetings are now better attended and the intercession is heart-felt rather than dutiful. Perhaps we are discovering that in this place of weakness we are closer to revival than in that place of apparent strength and fertility. In the words of Jesus: Blessed are the poor in spirit, for theirs is the kingdom of heaven (Matthew 5:3).

Britain and the USA 1739

Prior to the Great Awakening, Britain and North America were spiritually arid. Perhaps as few as five per cent of the British population were regularly attending church. "What is the present characteristic of the English nation?" John Wesley inquired. "It is ungodliness… Ungodliness is our universal, our constant, our peculiar character."[31]

It is easy to assume that revival was somehow easier in previous generations and it can be hard to find faith for a move of God in today's complex world. Yet in fact the great eighteenth century awakenings took place in times that were at least as dark as our own. In Britain no more than five Members of Parliament even attended church, and schools existed only for the elite. One humourous rumour suggested that parliament was planning to remove the word 'not' from the Ten Commandments and to add it to the Creeds instead! A form of Mafia was intimidating the populace and few people dared travel after dark without an armed guard. Conditions in the prisons were so appalling that many prisoners died there. Gin shops in London invited the public to "get drunk for a penny, or dead drunk for two pence and straw to lie on till the drunken stupor was gone."[32]

The prevailing attitudes of godless hedonism have many striking parallels with contemporary culture. "The dawn of the eighteenth century was a time of material prosperity in England… it was a day of luxury, dishonesty, speculation and extravagance… there was an anarchic spirit, infidelity was seen as trendy… the church was discredited… it seemed helpless… The ministry was largely corrupt… it was hard to find a sound gospel preacher anywhere in London. The Sabbath was a day of general carousing. Public blasphemy was common. Current literature and common conversation was lascivious and corrupt. God was openly defied. The outlook was dark indeed. Here and there a few godly men and women were crying unto God for reformation and revival. Then… three men were born in one year, 1703: John Wesley in England, Gilbert Tennent in Ireland and Jonathan Edwards in Massachusetts. Eleven years later George Whitefield was born. These four men were the human agents of the great spiritual awakening that broke like a storm over England and America just two hundred years ago."[33]

China 1948

Virtually every revival account is a story of God visiting the wilderness. In 1948 Mao Tse Tung, having seized power in China, expelled all Christian missionaries. The world watched helplessly, expecting the struggling Chinese church to die. Instead, out of such weakness, God showed his power and one of the greatest miracles of the twentieth century unfolded before us. Today there are more committed Christians in Communist China than signed up members of the Communist Party. In an article entitled *The Great Awakening — China's Christian revival*, the magazine *Asia Week* described it as "one of the most dramatic revivals in the history of Christianity."

Scotland 1949

Before the Hebridean awakening the Christians "came to an end of all human resources."[34] They knew that their churches were dry, their community was parched and their souls were thirsty for something more. There was nothing they could do but pray for a miracle, claiming God's promise to pour water on the thirsty land, and streams on the dry ground (Isaiah 44:3).

Argentina 1981

Many leaders in the remarkable Argentinean awakening trace its genesis to the day on which British Armed Forces sank the *General Belgrano* off the Falkland Islands. They believe that on that day the pride of their nation was shattered and out of their corporate pain and grief came God's healing life and power.

If we are to see an explosion of God's power in our time and nation, it will probably appear first in the desert because revival does not come as the climax of a triumphalistic crescendo, but rather as the gracious gift of God in response to the desperate cries of his people. When revival comes, it will almost certainly take us by surprise!

This is a vital lesson for the comfortable western church to learn, for while gospel fires sweep through much of the under-developed world, we experience spiritual famine. Their churches pulsate with life and supernatural power, while we have full bellies and empty hearts. We find ourselves materially comfortable and technologically advanced, insured against all life's eventualities (as if money can dull death's sting), pampered with pension schemes and three square meals a day, while our population lies emaciated and malnourished in its own filth.

Just two hundred years after Wesley, Britain is again materially wealthy and morally depraved. In such a climate the godly must take very seriously their responsibility to "prepare the way of the Lord", since it is in just such a wasteland that the Lord is likely to appear.

The return of Jesus

Isaiah's prophecy about a desert highway prepared for the King will only be realised fully when Jesus returns. It was partially fulfilled when God's people returned to Jerusalem from exile in Babylon, and then as John the Baptist prepared the way for the arrival of his cousin Jesus. But this prophetic word still hangs over us, unresolved, resonating with our spirits as we look for its fulfilment at the Second Coming of Christ the King. Ultimately, we long for revival because we long for the return of our Lord and friend, Jesus.

Former government minister Virginia Bottomley announced that the Second Coming of Jesus was a myth. In response to such cynicism the church has a prophetic mandate, once carried by John the Baptist, to cry out in these twenty-first century wastelands: "Get ready, the King *is* returning, remove the obstacles, purify yourselves." On his previous visit Jesus came on a donkey and his highway was just a dusty road, yet he changed the course of history. But this time his highway will be the holiness of his people: our prayers, our sacrifice, that irresistible combustion between his blood and our testimony. And this time he will ride on the clouds, every knee will bow and with loud cries and trumpets sounding the curtain will drop on history. I rather fancy kneeling next to Virginia Bottomley on that day…

What are we waiting for?

Exhausted Christians often find comfort in the last few verses of Isaiah 40: *Those who wait on the Lord will renew their strength…* However, it is easy to miss the context of this wonderful verse: Isaiah 40 is a chapter about the great coming of the King. It begins with the voice of one calling: *In the desert prepare the way for the Lord*, and it ends with an exhortation to *wait on the Lord*. What then, is it that renews my strength until I soar with the eagles? It is not just meditating on a Christian poster or listening to the latest "Worship to Whale Music" CD. My strength is renewed as I actively await my Master's return. We tend to think of waiting as a passive act: something one does in a bus queue or a doctor's surgery. But phrases like "waiting on the Lord" and "renewing our strength" are active, not passive. In fact the Hebrew word for renewing could literally describe swapping clothes with God, actively exchanging our weakness for his strength and beauty.

This big picture, the ultimate horizon of Christ's return, is so easy to forget amid the daily routines of life. As a result we can lose perspective, getting discouraged and run-down. At such times the stress of opposition and the struggle with sin just don't seem worth the effort and we can find ourselves losing hope in the desert. But in such moments we must remember that this life is not our home and that sin and suffering will evaporate like the mist on a summer dawn. On that day we will look Jesus in the eye knowing that the long, weary race has been run and we've made it home to be with him forever. This is the vision that renews strength. Lives lived in such certainty will pulse with the energy of heaven. That is why the New Testament writers repeatedly exhort persecuted churches to look beyond their suffering to the day of Christ's return. Two thousand years later this is still the ultimate longing that revitalises our strength and faith. The hope of Jesus' return is not just a vague get-out clause for a miserable church, but a certainty which we must grasp.

There is a great power in this hope for those, like me, who often feel discouraged and exhausted and occasionally get tempted to give up. As we consider revival, there is an excitement, a fresh energy and vision, the renewal of what David calls *a willing spirit to sustain me* (Psalm 51:12), and a release of faith because it brings the sure promise of the coming King.

> *A voice of one calling: "In the desert prepare the way for the Lord, make straight in the wilderness a highway for our God…" He gives strength and increases the power of the weak. Even youths grow tired and weary, and young men stumble and fall; But those who hope in the Lord will renew their strength…*
>
> (Isaiah 40:3, 29-31)

CHAPTER 7

RADICAL HOLINESS

Answering the question, "How do you have a revival?" Gipsy Smith replied, "Kneel down and with a piece of chalk draw a complete circle all round you — and pray to God to send revival on everything inside the circle. Stay there until he answers and you will have a revival."

Motives

In preparing our hearts for revival, it is vital that we examine our motives. A respected Christian leader confessed that he had never done anything with completely pure motives. His honesty in dealing with his own heart and his humility in admitting this are a great example. The fact is that people rarely, if ever, have completely pure motives in any form of public ministry or in seeking any form of blessing.

A young man came to share his vision for a beach ministry with me. I tried to keep a straight face as he listed all the great advantages of such a focus. I nodded seriously as he described the strategy of accessing people while they are relaxing and have time to talk, his burden for the surfing community, the need for urban regeneration of seaside towns, the prophetic significance of sun-cream... And then, with a broad grin, he added "and life on a beach sounds a lot of fun to me!" His honesty was refreshing and caused me to take him more seriously, not less.

Some people wait around for pure motivation but in their striving for perfection never actually do anything! We were planting a church into a new and exciting situation and one girl spent weeks praying about whether she should join us. Finally she rang and said that she had decided not to come. My wife was disappointed and asked her why. She said, "Well, I think my motives would be wrong. I love the place, I feel a burden for the people and worst of all, my boyfriend will be there". Fortunately we quickly talked her round!

Of course, we must seek holiness in every area of our motivation, but part of being tough on wrong motives will be admitting them to God and to our friends; after all this is what repentance is all about. Before preaching I often talk through with God the fact that I want to glorify him. I pray that people will focus not on me but on him, and that they will leave impressed by God's Word rather than my talk. However I also have to admit that there is a part of me that wants to be liked, appreciated and popular and would prefer not to get stoned on this particular occasion.

The trouble with revival is that it is such an enormous blessing that the scope for pride, selfish motivation, abuse of power, religious bigotry, competitiveness and hypocrisy is epic. Some businessmen in the Christian market will become millionaires practically overnight if revival breaks out. Other Christians will find themselves catapulted into the spotlight in their localities or onto national platforms of influence. Never is the demand for radical holiness so great as at times like these. No wonder God purifies the church before he impacts the world. Revival is a dangerous minefield for hearts that are not utterly broken before God — as Ananias and Sapphira found out. R. A. Torrey noted this capacity for wrong motivation: "Many prayers for revival are purely selfish. The churches desire revivals in order that the membership may be increased, in order that the church may have a position of more power and influence."[35]

There is a grave human tendency to love the blessing more than the one who blesses, to put the gift in the limelight and leave the giver in the twilight. In seeking God for revival, revival can all too easily become the god. Hosea exhorts us to *seek the Lord until he comes and showers righteousness on you* (Hosea 10:12). But we tend to reverse the emphasis and seek showers of righteousness until the Lord comes. The glory of the Lord must remain our priority, our desire and our motivation throughout.

Finney said that revival simply consists in obeying God, and one of the best measures of motive remains active obedience (rather than introspective self-analysis). The Lord calls us to take action against wrong motives, confessing them to others, and repenting of the "good we have not done".[36] How many people, when convicted of prayerlessness, read a book about prayer rather than simply praying! God speaks to them about their prayer life and so they share the word with a friend, testify to their situation and even ask for prayer for their prayer-problem, when all they need to do is kneel. Is God challenging you about timidity? Then learn the lesson of Moses: open your mouth and speak. Is your problem pride? Then humble yourself and God will raise you up. In the words of the Nike advertising slogan, whatever it is that God is challenging you to do: "Just do it!"

Suicide

A friend of mine was at a large work do in London conversing with an elegant lady at the bar. As the conversation progressed she commented on the number of people he seemed to know in his home town. Now Ian had prayed for an opportunity to mention Jesus that night but, as he later confessed, he generally pops his little light under the largest available bushel. He could respond to her comment in two ways: option one — "I went to school there"; option two — "I'm part of a church there". With a deep breath he mentioned church and was amazed by her response: "Oh you must tell me *all* about Christianity — I'm looking for a religion at the moment!"

In Jesus' day many people were also looking for a religion, and were attracted by the monotheism and morality of Judaism (though somewhat deterred, I imagine, by the prospect of circumcision). These seekers would worship at the synagogue and even visit Jerusalem for the Passover, without actually *converting* to Judaism.

Some Greeks like this went to see Philip one day and asked him to arrange an interview with Jesus (John 12:21). Perhaps they had been in the crowd waving palm leaves and shouting "Hosanna!" as he rode into town. Undoubtedly they had heard rumours about the miracles and healings and the resurrection of Lazarus from the dead. Understandably they were keen to meet the miracle man.

When Jesus heard that even the Greeks were coming to see him, he said an interesting thing: *The hour has come for the Son of man to be glorified* (John 12:23). Now Jesus might appear to be saying, "The hour has come for a little recognition. At last my ministry has gone truly international! A little glory for the Son of Man is long overdue." A fair comment when you remember that he had just raised Lazarus from the dead, his feet had been anointed with Chanel No.5 at a dinner party, and adoring crowds had cheered "Hosanna!" when he rode into town. Even his enemies were pointing out that *the whole world has gone after him* (John 12:19). And now, to cap it all, international visitors were requesting an audience. No wonder, one might think, Jesus says that *the hour has come for the Son of Man to be glorified.*

But Jesus is not referring to the world's glory.

The perfume with which he had been anointed was not only a symbol of festivity, it was also a ritual of burial. Those cheering crowds would soon change their cries of "Hosanna" to the darkest utterance of human history, "Crucify him..."

Clearly, this is not the glory of presidents and celebrities. It is not the sparkling company and stretch-limousine-luxury of Oscar night. It is the glory of the cross. Jesus states it so clearly: *The hour has come for the Son of Man to be glorified. I tell you the truth, unless a grain of wheat falls to the ground and dies it remains only a single seed. But if it dies, it produces many seeds* (John 12:24). In this upside-down Kingdom, the only road to glory is death. And if this was true for Jesus, how much more is it so for us?

The price of revival, the price of glory and the price of spiritual success is life on the altar and death to self. Daily, minute by minute in a thousand different ways, we must choose to sacrifice ourselves. I'm not talking about spiritual resignation or apathy, however — "Oh well, it's not up to me, I'm just a helpless old corpse on the altar." I'm talking about the deliberate daily suicide of actually picking up your cross, sitting in the electric chair, raising the revolver and following Jesus. This is ultimate trust, complete surrender and true freedom.

Jesus sweated blood, wrestling with his human survival instinct and fear of pain before he could pray "Not my will but yours." Even he struggled with the temptation to give up: "*Now my heart is troubled, and what shall I say? 'Father save me from this hour?' No, it was for this very reason I came. Father glorify your name!*" (John 12:27).

Jesus, who knew the exhilaration, the freedom and the energy of complete sinlessness chose to become sin. He was stripped naked and hung up to die. Such glory. When God offers to lift you up and draw people to you, think most carefully before accepting. In a century that has known more martyrs than the previous nineteen combined, their blood testifies loud and clear to the fact that revival glory walks hand in hand with persecution and pain.

My wife visited Ethiopia with a team to participate in a large Christian conference. One evening she received a prophetic word from God for one of the young women, and enthusiastically told her that God was calling her into leadership. To Samie's surprise the woman's face fell and she whispered "I'll have to think about it." The next day she returned with a lighter expression and announced "I have decided to accept God's word for me; I am willing to lead," adding quietly "I am willing to die." In an instant Samie realised the implication of her words. This woman came from the south of the country where church leaders risk imprisonment and even death. I wonder how many people would sign up for our leadership training courses in such an environment?

At the age of twenty-two a young man named Jim Elliot wrote some prophetic words in his diary: "He is no fool who gives what he cannot keep to gain what he cannot lose". Seven years later he was killed by the Auca Indians, a stone age tribe he had been seeking to love with the gospel. Most of us will never be called to lay down our lives literally, but we are all called to die to ourselves continually, in a million trivial ways, and this is the price of revival. Duncan Campbell experienced the cost of such blessing first hand and asks a searching question of us: "Is God hiding himself because we are unwilling to face the implications of the cross? We want revival but are we willing to pay the price? That price is death to the self-life. This surely is the place of victory and the price of revival. For the sake of our Lord, for the sake of perishing souls and the crown rights of our Redeemer, let us face the cross, and in the strength of his grace go through."

Dealing with sin

If we want to be used by God in revival we will have to be brutal with our sin. "The fact is", wrote Charles Finney, "that Christians are more to blame for not being revived than sinners are for not being converted."[37]

Robert Murray McCheyne led a church in Dundee, Scotland from the age of twenty-two to twenty-nine when he died. During this time God used him in a remarkable revival. All around him people were experiencing God, sinners were repenting, there were signs and wonders and the whole city was clamouring for his attention. The demands placed upon this young man's time must have been colossal as he preached and ministered from dawn to dusk. But in the midst of this revival McCheyne wrote something so profoundly simple it almost took my breath away when first I read it. He said, "My people's greatest need is my personal holiness."

Crowds were looking to him for guidance, doctrine and care and the angels were doubtless cheering him on. But this humble man realised that such anointing was not flowing from his pulpit (though hundreds responded), nor was it flowing from his prayer-life (though countless prayers were answered). The people's greatest need was not teaching, strategy, or even leadership at such a crucial time. Amidst so much grave need, the most pressing demand of all remained McCheyne's personal purity. He had discovered that the anointing would flow from God through him unhindered as long as he maintained private holiness. But should he neglect his love-life with God, should pride creep in or his prayer life wane, the revival flow would be obstructed and possibly even stopped.

When God begins to purify and refine his church exposing darkness and disturbing complacency; when God's people will no longer tolerate sin in their midst you can be fairly sure that a reviving work has begun.

Confession

It is said of Charles Finney that he never preached forgiveness until his audience was so ashamed of their sin that they could no longer meet his gaze. At times of revival there is an acute sensitivity to sin. Two of my closest friends visited the revival in Pensacola, Florida. On their return we gathered the congregation and for half an hour they shared what they had seen. One of them confessed that after twelve years as a Christian and eight years in full-time church leadership, God had so challenged him about his own compromise that it was like being born again, again. The simple truth had impacted him profoundly that "sin is not an option". He had not been involved in terrible immorality or deliberate disobedience, but he had grown painfully aware of areas of subtle compromise and excuses that had been given the credibility of time until they even convinced his own conscience.

As they finished speaking a very great seriousness fell on that room and young people spontaneously began to stand up and publicly confess sin, often with tears. I had never witnessed anything like it in all my life. For well over an hour person after person took the microphone and confessed. There were deep and profound sins that required remarkable honesty. Some confessed attitudes and actions which, in the past, might have seemed trivial but somehow were no longer acceptable. One professional man confessed that before moving to the area he had been sacked from his job and had been too ashamed to ever admit it to anyone here in his new church family. For years he felt he had been covering up. As each person left the microphone others would gather round and minister the peace and forgiveness of God to them.

In that single evening we saw more pastoral breakthrough with certain individuals than had been achieved by years of care. The Bible has since come to life in a new way for many. Passages of scripture that for years I had ignored or glossed over began to gnaw at me. The book of James, that Luther famously wanted to remove from the canon, particularly challenged me. The verse about confessing sin took on new relevance: *Therefore, confess your sins to each other and pray for each other so that you may healed* (James 5:16). We had certainly felt some of the power of such confession.

Perhaps most challenging of all is James' insistence on labelling apathy and passivity as sin: *Anyone, then, who knows the good he ought to do and doesn't do it, sins* (James 4:17). In evangelism, in caring for the poor, in words that needed to be said and were not, in so many sins of neutrality, I was convicted of my disobedience (Anglicans helpfully describe these as sins of omission). For several days I wrestled with God as he convicted me of specific attitudes. There were people I had to see and actions I had to take. But bit by bit I was finding a new passion and freedom in Christ.

Conviction vs. condemnation

It is very important that we don't confuse such seasons of conviction (which are evidently from God) with feelings of condemnation (which are from Satan, the Accuser). After all, Paul clearly told the Romans that *There is now no condemnation for those who are in Christ Jesus* (Romans 8:1). While condemnation inflicts aimless sensations of unworthiness and inadequacy, conviction always points to specific areas of sin and calls for remedial action. God is always specific against sin, like a surgeon who goes straight to the area of sickness and with infinite precision cuts it out. Sadly, many Christians find it much easier to accept guilt and condemnation than they do forgiveness and freedom.

Condemnation	Conviction
• From the Accuser and Father of lies	• From God, the Truth and the Light
• A vague sense of guilt or unworthiness that depresses you into denying the power of the cross for forgiveness	• Spotlights a specific sin and inspires you to approach the cross for forgiveness
• The fruit is bondage and despair	• The fruit is freedom and health

One of the specific things that God convicted me of during this time was living a prayerless life. I argued for a while, informing God — in case it had slipped his mind — that I conversed with him on a regular basis. But deep down I knew that it was true. God had often challenged me to pray more and at a deeper level in private and I had either ignored that challenge or done it for a few days before returning to normal. I stood up and confessed this to the congregation, which is embarrassing when you're supposed to be a mature, spiritual leader. I told them that I needed to get up earlier each day to make prayer a priority.

Now I like sleeping. I also hate all forms of bodily deprivation from cold showers and hard exercise to fasting. I'm certainly not someone who jumps cheerfully out of bed at five each morning singing Handel's *Messiah* and skips lightly downstairs to evangelise the milkman. But specific conviction requires a specific response. So I began to set two alarm-clocks at night; one by my bed ready for the usual assault and the other set five minutes later down the hallway outside the bedroom of our grumpiest lodger. This second alarm clock is shaped like a duck and cock-a-doodle-doos loud enough to break windows and it was only the insatiable desire to strangle that duck each morning before the lodger awoke that propelled me from my bed to pray.

True holiness

People tend to associate holiness with sobriety and heaviness, but this is not what it means to be filled with God's Spirit of life and love. It is appropriate for convicted sinners to be bowed down with grief for a while but such dismay is temporary and a means to an end. As we cry out to God he forgives us and makes us holy. In revival, tears lead to celebration and heaviness of spirit soon becomes rejoicing. Holiness is joyful, dynamic and powerfully magnetic. God's objective in convicting his church is never to depress us or crush us but to liberate us from the sin that robs us of our humanity.

True humanity is holy; set apart for its Creator. In the Garden of Eden, Adam and Eve were "set apart" in intimate friendship with God, existing in order to enjoy paradise with him. He would walk and talk with them each day until sin robbed them of this intimate birthright. But the Gospel proclaims the incredible news that humanity can rediscover the joy of Eden through the holiness that Christ gives us. Thus, holiness is about being truly alive, truly human, and does not call for a perpetual abstention from pleasure. God loves life and calls us to celebrate our humanity in relationship with him. Holiness has nothing to do with draining the humanity from our lives.

> *Christian faith… never doubts for a moment that it is a great and glorious thing to be a human being. Faith can find a place, though not without criticism, for all the wonderful achievements of the human race in society, in culture, in art, even in the somewhat tarnished glories of technical civilisation. But at the same time it looks with wide-open and dispassionate eyes on the squalor, the contradictions, the self-destroying*

absurdity of human existence. By our own ingenuity we have built up a brave new world of our own invention and now, like a child tired of its toys, we seem to be set on destroying it and with it the whole race of which we are a part. In vision and aspiration man's head touches the heavens, but his feet stand firmly in the ooze and slime of primeval chaos. As Pascal saw clearly, we cannot understand man unless we consider him in both his greatness and his misery. But, having made an exhaustive inventory of the misery, Christian faith still affirms that it is a good thing to be a human being.[38]

Tragically, however, religious people down the ages have given holiness a bad name:

- A Sicilian monk named Conor existed for thirty years on one meal per week because he thought this would make him holy. I can't think of anything less akin to God's creation intention for humanity than self starvation.
- A man names Sisoes spent the night on a jutting crag so that if he fell asleep he would fall to his death.

Some people have adopted the principle "the dirtier the holier", sacrificing personal hygiene because they thought it pleased God:

- Simon Stylites was considered very holy because "his body dropped vermin as he walked."
- A man named Anthony never changed his vest or washed his feet.
- At the age of sixty the virgin Silvania boasted that after her conversion she never allowed water to touch her, except the tips of her fingers, despite medical advice.[39] And when the Roman lady Melania lost her husband and two of her three sons in a single week she thanked God: "More easily can I serve thee, O Lord, in that thou hast relieved me of so great a burden."

At times people would go to the most terrible extremes in their distorted perceptions of holiness. A father called Mucius entered a monastery with his eight-year-old son. The monks systematically beat the boy to test Mucius but we are told "The love of Christ conquered, nor did he grieve over the lad's injuries." Such tragic religion breaks the very heart of God and serves as nothing but a mockery of the gospel.

Even the great John Wesley, in his admirable work establishing schools, forbade the children from playing because he considered such behaviour unspiritual.[40]

Satan loves to distort our understanding of holiness because it is such a key to God's dream for our lives. Jesus said *The thief comes only to steal and kill and destroy; I have come that they may have life, and have it to the full* (John 10:10).

The route to revival

I had to discover the hard way that the only route to revival leads through the refiner's fire. I had been through a very dry period, and God seemed a million miles away. My girlfriend had ended our relationship, leaving me bruised with rejection. School friends had gone away to University leaving me lonely and I found myself cleaning toilets for a living. Worst of all I felt far away from my heavenly Father. In the midst of these difficult months of silence God suddenly spoke. It was Christmas time and I was sorting through some cards on a mantle-piece when a Bible verse on one of them seemed to jump off the page: *If you spend yourselves on behalf of the hungry and satisfy the needs of the oppressed, then your light will rise in the darkness, and your night will become like noonday* (Isaiah 58:10).

The words had a profound impact on me. My heart was inexplicably racing. I would classify it as one of the few occasions when I have heard God unmistakably. If everyone else had told me that I was mistaken I would still have been quite sure that I was not and that God was telling me to go to the hungry and oppressed. In the months that followed I explored the options and ended up in Hong Kong working with Jackie Pullinger's ministry to heroin-addicts and street-sleepers.

I had heard remarkable stories of what God was doing through Jackie. I knew that miraculous healings were taking place on a daily basis and that many were being converted. It was intoxicating stuff, and with typical pomp I announced to my friends that I was going to Hong Kong to pick up the secrets of revival. On my return I would simply get one started in my home town before progressing to Surrey, England and Europe.

I arrived in Hong Kong to discover that the stories were true. I will never forget the eyes of a blind lady who had received her sight, or aged junkies who had found new life in Christ. But instead of pumping me up with excitement, God began to break me down. I was surrounded by people who were so much more like Jesus than me that I felt ashamed. I developed a craving for Christ that consumed me and would often spend my day off locked in a tiny room, crying and asking God to change me. Revival was no longer the issue, signs and wonders were not my focus, my obsession was to know Christ beyond all else. When I returned to the UK people were amazed by how much God had humbled, broken and changed me. And, of course, that was the biggest miracle of all.

Jesus made it clear that our only responsibility as his followers is to love the Father and that our Christian C.V. will not remotely impress him on Judgment Day. *Not everyone who says to me "Lord, Lord", will enter the Kingdom of Heaven, but only he who does the will of my Father who is in heaven. Many will say to me on that day, "Lord, Lord, did we not prophesy in your name, and in your name drive out many demons and perform many miracles?" Then I will tell them plainly, "I never knew you. Away from me you evildoers!"* (Matthew 7:21-28). It is possible to be used dynamically in revival and yet be far from Jesus.

In the family business

The Queen describes the task of reigning over the United Kingdom as "the family business". But the King of Kings is not the same. God is not consumed with "the family business" but just with the family. You can serve him faithfully and even brilliantly as your Managing Director, furthering his interests on earth, and yet fail to inherit the very Kingdom you have spent your life extending. The principle is simple: family members inherit, employees do not.

No wonder God was more concerned about changing my heart in Hong Kong than fulfilling my vision. After all, as Gerald Coates has observed: "God has designed us to be human *beings*, not human *doings*". It is infinitely more important to our Father that we live as his children than that we accrue lists of spiritual credit. Holiness means being liberated from everything that imprisons and cheapens us so that we can run to the open arms of our Creator, and it is only ever there in that moment of embrace that we find our true identity and the certainty of our inheritance.

A legacy of love

When my father died I inherited some money. I spent it on a camera, which was later stolen by a drug-addict and doubtless sold for a pittance. But because I loved my father the money was the least of my inheritance. I had inherited riches far more precious than cash: a jumper that always reminds me of him, the spiritual legacy of his prayers, even some of his physical mannerisms and features.

When Christians talk about our inheritance as God's sons, we all too easily focus upon gifts that are far less important than the sheer joy of being his children and growing to resemble him more with each passing year. If my main desire had been to inherit Dad's money he would rightly have been hurt and angry.

On the Final Day there will be people who have cashed in their inheritance by casting out demons or healing the sick, without ever receiving or returning the love behind it. These power-gifts are available to us and are given in order that we might use them, but ultimately they will pass away — just like my inherited cash. It is only the reality of "knowing" the Father that will carry us beyond death into his presence.

If the predictions are correct remarkable days are coming. It may well be that over the coming years our influence will increase nationally. There may be lights ahead that leave us dazed. Dreams may come true as loved ones find Christ and as corruption is exposed. I for one, am praying for such days with all my heart. But if such wonders should grace our lifetime, let us fix our eyes resolutely on Jesus and let us live as children of heaven.

The heart of the matter

True holiness, then, has little to do with exterior appearance or Christian achievement. It is an expression of our relationship with our Father. A good friend used to drink eight pints of beer a night. When he became a Christian he managed to cut this down to four. Now some people might look judgmentally at a Christian drinking four pints of beer in a single night, but God saw his heart and loved it. Needless to say the total continued to decrease!

The church can all too easily judge holiness superficially. We can be more concerned about cleaning up the exterior of a new Christian to make them blend in respectably as quickly as possible, than addressing the heart issues. I heard about a church where an enthusiastic new convert stood up to testify to God's goodness, but carelessly swore in the process. The majority of the congregation was unable to hear the heart behind the swear word and escorted him out of the building.

Jesus often exposed the fallacy that everyone who appears holy is in fact holy, and revealed that some people who are labelled sinners are actually at the heart of his Kingdom. The rich young ruler, for instance, had managed to keep every single commandment and most churches today would hand him a covenant form before he could blink. But Jesus saw the materialism that motivated him and watched him walk away. He memorably denounced the Pharisees as whitewashed tombs: gleaming white on the outside but filthy internally. But then he welcomed a promiscuous woman's caress because he saw the purity of her motives. Holiness, it should be noted, is rarely synonymous with respectability.

Holiness first

Preparation for revival begins with purity of heart; ridding ourselves of sin and setting ourselves apart for God. Joshua told the people of Israel before entering the Promised Land: *Consecrate yourselves for tomorrow the Lord will do amazing things among you* (Joshua 3:3). Consecration and expectation go hand in hand. When a people sets itself apart for the Lord, he will soon move in remarkable ways.

In 1987 a member of John Wimber's Vineyard team gave a significant prophetic word, predicting that God was going to send two winds upon the church. The first wind "shall be named *Holiness unto the Lord*" and it will blow through every church, every Christian institution and every ministry bringing holiness. Some people would be "tempted to brand this as a work of Satan but this is my wind. I cannot tolerate my church in its present form nor will I tolerate it... with tornado force it will come and appear to leave devastation but the word of the Lord comes and says: 'Turn your face into the wind and let it blow, for only that which is not of me shall be devastated.

You must see this as necessary... in my first wind that is upon you now I will blow out pride, lust, greed, competition, jealousy and you will feel devastated. But haven't you read "Blessed are the poor in Spirit because theirs is the Kingdom of Heaven"?'"

Just months later the sin of various television evangelists and other public ministries exploded into the media. God continues to purify his church. The Toronto blessing has shaken God's people powerfully (and literally!). Similarly, the message flowing from Pensacola is one of repentance and righteousness. Perhaps these are among the winds of holiness.

The second wind, he prophesied, would be called *The Kingdom of God.* "It shall bring my power. The supernatural shall come in that wind... fear of God shall fall on the nation... You have longed for revival and a return to the miraculous and the supernatural. You and your generations shall see it... The church of this nation cannot contain my power in its present form. But as it turns to the wind of the holiness of God it shall be purged and changed to contain my glory. This is the judgment that has begun at the house of God but it is not the end. When the second wind has come and brought in my harvest then shall the end come."

This prophetic word echoes the biblical theme of holiness preceding revival, and should inspire us to welcome the purifying wind of holiness into our lives and our churches in preparation for the wind of the Kingdom, the hurricane of revival. Significantly the prophecy warns that there will be many who want to enjoy the second wind of the harvest but cannot, because they will have hardened their hearts against the first wind, the shaking.

In this chapter we have addressed the human heart, seeing that it is only as God refines our motives and as we surrender ourselves completely to him, that revival can take root in our lives. A heart set apart for Jesus in this way will inevitably begin to carry his burdens, longing that his will be done on earth as it is in heaven. A holy heart is a praying heart and that is where we must now turn the spotlight.

CHAPTER 8

PRAYER KEY 1: HUMILITY & FAITH

At the heart of every revival is the spirit of prayer.

Arthur Wallis

One of the most remarkable events of the eighteenth century occurred on 13th August 1727. The Spirit of God fell with incredible power upon a Moravian prayer meeting in Herrnhut, Saxony (modern-day Germany). So great was this outpouring that the meeting continued for a hundred years without stopping. Twenty-four men and twenty-four women determined that the flame of intercession should burn at the heart of their community continually, and so they divided themselves to pray in succession around the clock. The number of intercessors actually increased as the years rolled on, especially among the children, generating a power centre that radiated to the ends of the earth for more than a century.

More than one hundred evangelists were sent out from that small village in the twenty-five years following that momentous night, taking the gospel to most countries in Europe as well as the Americas, Asia and Africa. John Wesley was one of their many converts and "Mad Moravians", aflame with the gospel, kept on popping up in obscure contexts and far-flung countries like a delightful motif running through eighteenth century missions.

Twelve years later another prayer meeting detonated an even bigger explosion as the Wesley brothers, their friend George Whitefield and others (including, predictably, a Moravian) met in Fetter Lane, London. God visited that unsuspecting group in such glory that the destiny of the eighteenth century was rewritten in a matter of minutes.

Ask for it

Prayer has been the universal ingredient common to every revival down the ages and across the world. In fact if you want a formula for revival it is probably as simple as "ask God for it". In 1904 a Wiltshire evangelist visited a meeting of the Welsh revival. He stood up and said "Friends, I have journeyed into Wales that I may learn the secret of the Welsh Revival!" Evan Roberts jumped to his feet and replied: "My Brother — there is no secret! Ask and ye shall receive."

According to the eminent theologian Edwin Orr, the years 1900 to 1910 hosted the greatest worldwide awakening in human history. With the benefit of hindsight we can see that it all began with prayer on a massive scale before the turn of the century. Significant prayer movements were fanned into flame at the Moody Bible Institute in Chicago, the Keswick Convention in England and in parts of India, the Far East, Africa and Latin America. These intercessors did not fully understand the scale of prayer that God was calling forth, but together laid the foundations for the revival decade. This should challenge us to pray but also thrill us with excitement for "never in Christian history has there been such a longing for renewal in so many parts of the world and by people from so many denominational backgrounds as there is today"[41]

Our current potential in prayer is unlimited and if we will take it seriously, we could be heading for an international explosion of God's power of unparalleled dimensions. The fact is that right now there is more power waiting to be unleashed on the world by the praying church than by the nuclear capabilities of world superpowers; it is a truly awesome responsibility.

The Hebridean awakening began in focused and faith-filled prayer. On one occasion, in the village of Arnol, the house in which they were praying physically shook. Arthur Wallis reflects that prayer was equally central to Pentecost: "Let it be burned upon our hearts by the Spirit of God that this mighty movement that turned the world upside down was not only born out of prayer, but that it brought forth prayer, and was maintained by prayer."[30]

The promise of revival

The great revival preacher Evan Roberts began working, like many Welshmen, as a coal miner. Everywhere he went he carried a Welsh Bible which had been scorched in a mine explosion from which he escaped unharmed. Prophetically, the fire had burned the pages of 2 Chronicles 6, the passage in which Solomon as a young man prays for revival. It is in the following chapter that God makes his reply: *If my people, who are called by my name, will humble themselves and pray and seek my face and turn from their wicked ways, then I will hear from heaven and will forgive their sins and heal their land* (2 Chronicles 7:14).

The one true God does not change his mind or water down such promises and they are as certain today as they have ever been. If we will only take him at his word and fulfil our obligation to repent and humbly pray, God guarantees revival. In the next three chapters we will look at the four vital prayer-keys which unlock revival.

- Praying with Humility
- Praying with Faith
- Persevering in Prayer
- Intercessory Prayer

Praying with Humility

If my people... will humble themselves... It takes humility to bend the knee and pray. Proud hearts are less inclined to pray because deep down they suspect that they can achieve the desired result independently and when they do pray, it can appear more like approaching God for his rubber-stamp upon their plans rather than seeking his face. Pride (which overestimates self) and unbelief (which underestimates God) tempt us to think that time spent in prayer could be more usefully deployed actually *doing* something. But when we come to the Lord in brokenness, helplessness and dependency we can be sure that he hears and acts. That is why Paul identifies a powerful Christian as one who embraces weakness (2 Corinthians 12:9).

It is ironic that pride actually enforces weakness, robbing us of ultimate power because it keeps us from our knees. When a newborn baby lies on its back and cries, its deepest human instincts are being stirred. It is crying out for food, for love, for its mother without whom it will die. This is a picture of the dependency and humility that stirs God's heart. We seek God's face because we are helpless like a newborn baby without him. But as we grow older it takes increasing humility to admit such dependency. This is just one reason why children are closer to the Kingdom of Heaven than adults; they know how to need.

Learning to need

A friend who is going through terrible pain at the moment recently commented, "I am more and more convinced that people only really pray when they need to." I believe that statement to be profoundly true, although at first I reacted: "What about those with disciplined daily prayer-lives?" I objected, "Surely they pray even when things are fine?" But perhaps such people are just humble enough, or hurting enough, to have a consistent awareness of their need to pray. The fact is that those who are content also tend to be complacent in prayer, while those who suffer cry out to God.

I once knew a lady who had prayed for her non-Christian husband for years. She had tried every technique to witness to him without effect. Nothing, it seemed could penetrate his self-sufficient world. Then, one night, he came home and found that the house had been burgled and his family were away. Alone in his ransacked home that night he discovered his sense of need and gave his life to the Lord.

One of my best friends is soon to move with his young family to Brooklyn, New York to plant a new church. He is leaving behind close friends, his job and his security. These are vulnerable days as he says many goodbyes and prepares for the unknown but in such uncertainty he is finding God in a new way. His prayer times as he walks the beach have been injected with emotion. He has undoubtedly rediscovered his sense of need and it is giving impetus to his personal prayer-life.

So many public prayers involve listing off to God things he already knows, or even explaining points of theology to him! I'm all in favour of informality in prayer and I love it when people just pour out their hearts to God. But listen to someone praying with a profound sense of need and there is a raw pleading and a humble reverence springing from that heart-cry. A friend is dying and only God can heal; the money has run out and only God can provide; an unsaved parent is dead to Christ and only he can save them. This is the prayer of the humble heart. As long as we think we can achieve a particular result independently, we will pray shallow prayers, if we pray at all. But God is attentive to the prayers of *the poor in spirit… those who mourn… the meek… those who hunger and thirst for righteousness, for they will be filled* (Matthew 5:3-6). The prayer that triggers revival and the prayer that revival triggers will always be marked by humility and brokenness before God.

Praying with Faith

> *Much of our praying is nothing short of the laughing stock of devils; praying "God, you're the God of revival! You're the God of the impossible!" when we don't believe a word of it. If we did the miracle would happen. Oh my people, let's be frank and honest: He's not doing it! We are faced with this question: "Can these bones live? Can we really expect revival? Can God match this situation?"*[42]

More and more people are praying for revival and prayer-groups are multiplying. National and international initiatives gather hundreds of thousands of Christians in prayer and this is utterly thrilling. But Scripture clearly teaches that it is not so much the *quantity* of prayer but the *quality*; the depth, the perseverance, the humility and above all the faith behind it. We are probably all guilty at times of praying faithless prayers more akin to wishful thinking than actual spiritual authority. But no matter how impressive our prayers sound, without faith they are powerless and pointless like a gleaming sports car without an engine.

Faith in the faithfulness of God

Faith is the vital ingredient of the Christian life; Jesus would often distil complex situations down to the essence of faith, informing the sick, "Your faith has healed you" or rebuking people for their unbelief. The writer to the Hebrews says that without faith it is completely impossible to please God (Hebrews 11:6). The disciples approached the Lord one day and asked for more faith, but in reply

Jesus gently admonished them: *You don't need more faith. There is no "more" or "less" in faith. If you have a bare kernel of faith, say the size of a poppy seed, you could say to this sycamore tree, "Go jump in the lake," and it would do it.* (Luke 17:6 — Eugene Peterson's translation)

With our western quantitative mind sets we interpret this reference to *faith as small as a mustard seed* (NIV) as referring to an *amount* of faith necessary. We might think that our present quantity of faith is the size of a mere speck of dust and as a result we only see the occasional verruca healed, but that if we could somehow grow our faith to the size of a mustard seed then we would be able to rearrange the landscape.

But ironically this is the very mentality that Jesus is rebuking! He is saying that size doesn't matter. Miracles are not proportional to the quantity of faith because even the tiniest amount imaginable could shift a mountain. Lots more faith is not the answer to the mountains of cancer or evangelism. The key is not faith in a power formula, but faith in a powerful person. Jesus is saying that either you place your trust in him or you don't.[43] When I board an aeroplane I place my entire trust in the pilot's ability to do what I cannot do and fly that 'plane. It is not possible to hedge my bets, just in case, and keep one foot on the runway as we take off! I must either place my trust in the pilot, in which case I fly, or I can distrust the pilot and remain firmly on the ground, but there is no in-between. In the same way there is no sliding scale when it comes to faith.

Hudson Taylor, the great apostle to China, wrote "The issue is not greater faith, but faith in a great God."[44] If we lack faith, therefore, it is futile trying to stir it up from within. Instead we need a revelation of the greatness of God. When we discover that his name is Faithful, that his promises are sure and that he is utterly trustworthy it becomes easy to trust him. The first approach focuses on self to try to arouse faith, the second approach derives faith from the realisation that God really can be trusted. Focusing on quantities of faith as the answer to a situation makes faith out to be some kind of formula for manipulating reality (no matter how many Bible verses are woven into the equation). Such faith-formulae may even work, since there may well be an inherent, limited power in "mind over matter" that is neither demonic nor divine. For instance, there are authenticated reports of mothers lifting cars off their children after a road accident with apparently superhuman strength. Similarly, some Management Training Courses teach clients to run barefoot over red-hot coals simply by psyching themselves up. There is no burning to the feet because — like passing a finger through a flame — it is quite possible to do this apparently impossible act without harm. Yet one coal-runner commented "I now believe I can do almost anything." This has everything to do with faith but nothing whatsoever to do with Jesus. It is clearly not a faith that flows from the revelation of God's will. Even Christians may use faith equations based on Bible verses, to achieve real results that have little to do with Jesus. He actually warned us that many would succeed in performing miracles in his name without ever having known him (Matthew 7:23). Biblical faith has nothing to do with the power of positive thinking. It is faith in a person and not in a principle or technique and so we must be people whose faith is lodged firmly in the Word of God.

Jesus modelled God-focused faith perfectly: *I do nothing on my own but speak just what the Father has taught me…* (John 8:28). Here then is the key to Jesus' power: he lived his life focused upon the Father, saying only what he heard the Father saying and doing only what he saw the Father doing. Confronted by incurable illnesses, demonic manifestations or stormy seas Jesus fixed his eyes upon the Father. There is no cure in the illness, no freedom in the demoniac and no peace in the storm. But we put our hope in the higher reality that God is the God of health, freedom and peace. The issue therefore is not faith but focus. No wonder we are told to pray and seek God's face, for it is only as we look to him that we find faith for breakthrough.

If Peter had pulled out a video camera and filmed the scene as Jesus arrived at Jairus' house, we would have found the evidence conclusive: Jairus' daughter was indeed dead. We would see for ourselves the mourners in black, the mother pale and weeping and the corpse lifeless on the bed. But Jesus was watching another reality as he entered the house and announced with absolute certainty *She is not dead but asleep* (Matthew 9:24). In a matter of minutes the mourners discovered that Jesus, far from being deluded, was more in touch with reality than every single one of them because he kept his eyes fixed on heaven, *walking by faith, not by sight* (2 Corinthians 5:7).

Faith in the promises of God

> *All the mighty interceding of the ages that has ever shaken the Kingdom of darkness has been based upon the promises of God. Why should we expect God to do what he has not agreed to do?*[45]

It is because faith comes from knowing God that his promises are so vital, providing a foundation on which to base our faith. They assure us of his provision when we are in need, his love when we are lonely and his victory even when the material evidence appears to point to defeat. Materialism (the belief that matter is all that matters) is the greatest enemy of faith. Its inverted creed of "walk by sight and not by faith" will often contradict the promises of God's Word. When Christians live in an environment of materialism they find it hard to see the world with eyes of faith. But in non-materialistic cultures the most remarkable miracles consistently take place in answer to prayer. Our worship leader visited Nigeria and saw miracles in that environment that just don't happen here to the same degree. He even interviewed a man who had raised seven corpses from the dead. If matter is our ultimate focus then death is ultimate defeat. But if the resurrected Christ is our focus we can look beyond a corpse and see life, hope and victory.

Get real!

All this talk about "walking by faith rather than sight" and ignoring the physical evidence to trust God for something else, could be a ticket for super-spiritual unreality. I have known people to pray unsuccessfully for healing only to inform the suffering person "You have been healed... it's just the symptoms that remain"! This is completely ridiculous. The greatest gift that God wants to give to some Christians is not tongues or prophecy but common sense. I am not for one moment suggesting that we kiss our brains good-bye and deny blatant reality. In fact God-focused faith in not unreal, but is based upon firm evidence. As Finney put it: "Faith must have evidence. Without reason we have no right — and no obligation — to believe a thing will be done. Belief without evidence is fanaticism."[46]

Faith must be founded upon three vital pieces of evidence:

- the evidence of God's promises
- the evidence of circumstance
- the evidence of God's specific command.

Because these evidences are individually open to misapplication and misinterpretation we need to make ourselves accountable before praying over corpses, selling all our possessions or marrying the complete stranger in the third row! If we are honest, not many of us have an intimacy with the Father sufficient to declare with absolute certainty "she is not dead but sleeping", which is why we need to measure our inclinations against the Word of God, heeding common sense and the wise counsel of others.

When faith is based on evidence and applied accountably it does not need to be frightened of facts. If someone has been healed then the doctor will verify this, and until this has been done, vital medication should not normally be abandoned. When I offer to pray with a non Christian for healing I will always be honest about the possibility that it might not work. They invariably appreciate this honesty and reality, as well as the fact that I care enough to risk praying even though there is no guaranteed result.

We have seen in this chapter that our prayers for revival must be full of faith and that such faith only comes by taking God at his word and trusting his promises. Isaiah said that if we want to "soar on wings as eagles", riding the thermals of the Spirit, we must wait on God (Isaiah 40:31). Timing is everything. In fact without such watching and waiting, all our prayers and preparations will never get off the ground; we will resemble frantic turkeys flapping around clumsily, rather than the majestic eagles God intends. Nicky Gumbel recounts a vivid illustration of this point:

> *Eagles do not fly — if you mean by that the flapping of wings to propel them from one place to another. Other birds do that, but not eagles. They have an inborn ability to discern wind currents. They do not go anywhere until the right breeze comes along. When it comes, they just let go, born aloft by the wind. They do not have to flap their wings (how uncouth!) — eagles have the ability to lock their wings in place. All they do is ride the wind. Other birds are afraid of storms. Eagles love a storm. It forces them higher and higher and higher.*

Many Christians do their work for the Lord by the sweat of their brow. They join the cult of white knuckles. They really "work for God", like turkeys. Have you ever seen a turkey fly? They beat themselves into insensibility, propelling themselves across a farmyard. They cannot get more than three feet off the ground. Eagle Christians do not serve by the grit of their teeth or sweat of their brow. It is service by the power of God through the wind of the Holy Spirit — discerning his purpose and then going with it, not trying to get him to bless your mess.[47]

CHAPTER 9

PRAYER KEY 2: PERSEVERANCE

In the day of small things...

For most of us there is an enormous gulf between our aspirations in prayer and our present reality. But faith lives in the tension between these two extremes.

We live in a day of small things, yet dare to dream of revival. It is encouraging to note therefore that throughout scripture, faith-filled men and women have looked at acorns and perceived oak trees:

- Abraham looked at barren Sarah and trusted God for Isaac. He then looked at Isaac and perceived an entire nation.
- Joshua and Caleb returned from their spying mission, and while others described a land of giants, they placed their faith in God's insignificant nomadic people.
- David saw tiny stones and a simple sling and trusted God for the greatest victory in his nation's history.
- Simeon, standing in enemy-occupied Israel, after four hundred years of silence from heaven, saw a new-born baby and perceived the Messiah. The baby could not walk, talk or feed himself, yet by faith Simeon saw and knew.
- God himself took a few loaves and a fish... He picked a dozen rough necked men... He limited himself to a few hundred square miles of earth, to a short span of years and to a human

body before the age of the combustion engine, surgery or international communication. Ultimately, he limited his body to a couple of planks of wood on a dusty hill in the Middle East, and there the Creator died.

Insignificance. Small things. A nameless cripple healed, a long forgotten widow comforted, friends who were marginalised, faceless witnesses. Mundane stories of farmers and children and savings. These things veiled the most profound truths of the universe. Such a Saviour inspires faith in the day of small things.

God has made it clear that he prefers using the small and the insignificant to achieve his ends. He even considered Gideon's army too large for victory! I cannot think of a single example in scripture of a character called and used by God who was an obvious or a "strategic" choice. We should take great comfort, therefore, from the fact that the church today is such an eccentric and motley crew of social misfits. Jesus has always chosen friends like that.

Conspiracy of the insignificant

Gerald Coates calls the church "God's overwhelming minority", and Tom Sine describes the Kingdom as "a conspiracy of the insignificant."[48] We must learn to discern God's hand in the small and inconsequential. It is not that we settle for tiny churches and unanswered prayer, but rather that we are faithful in small things, perceiving the greater works of God despite our frustrations and discouragements. This is the measure of true faith; after all it doesn't take much faith to perceive revival once you're actually in it! But to stand by the tiniest trickle of hope and hear the roar of a great Niagara: that takes faith. In fact for any visionary the only alternative to terminal frustration is going to be faith that things can change.

Elijah was a man of great faith in an age of terrible discouragement. God's prophets had been persecuted into near oblivion and immorality ruled the land under Jezebel and her spineless husband Ahab. But after Elijah's victorious showdown with the prophets of Baal on Mount Carmel we read: *Ahab went off to eat and drink, while Elijah climbed to the top of Carmel, bent down to the ground and put his face between his knees* (1 Kings 18:42-44).

He knew that the fire of judgment, which had consumed his sacrifice, was only the first baptism. Now he prayed that God would lift the curse and send the baptism of rain that would terminate years of drought. The skies were blue and cloudless, yet Elijah's spirit could hear *the sound of heavy rain* (1 Kings 18:41). As he listened he prayed, sending his servant again and again to scan the horizon for even the smallest sign. At last the servant reported one insignificant cloud the size of a man's fist, and Elijah knew for certain that his prayers had been answered. This small, unimpressive cloud was enough to convince him that rain was coming, and it was coming fast.

Note two things in this story: first that Elijah sent his *servant* to look. Why did he not just open his eyes? I can only assume that it was because he needed to focus on a higher reality, he was listening with his spiritual ears to "the sound of a heavy rain" and could not afford to be distracted by the disconcerting fact of a cloudless sky.

Second, note that Elijah's faith predated the evidence: the formation of a tiny rain-cloud. He was not exercising faith for the remotely possible, having noticed the hint of rain materialising on the horizon. Elijah was trusting God for the entirely impossible, praying for rain when the sky was still clear. By the time that the cloud had actually appeared his job was already done! Although the sun was still shining Elijah rose from his knees immediately and began sprinting ahead of the imminent downpour.

Sometimes we scan the horizon for an indication of revival, and there is none. The slightest cloud would give us hope but burnished skies just mock our prayers for rain. Revival seems as distant and unlikely as snow on a summer day. But these are the occasions that demand faith and perseverance. At such times we will not find faith by searching the skies, or the newspapers for signs of hope. We will find faith by bowing with our heads between our knees as Elijah did, seeking God's face and claiming his promises. It is in that place of prayer, and only there, that we will find faith for the impossible.

I suspect that this is one of the reasons why Jesus so often rose early and sought out isolation to pray. Like Elijah he needed time to listen to the mighty rain of God's promises. He knew that the day ahead would confront him with impossible situations, unsolvable by the human mind. He needed first to tune in to the sights and sounds of heaven, to find the hope that rises above the horizon of human possibility. In these important moments before dawn, Jesus would seek his Father's face knowing that *With man this is impossible, but with God all things are possible* (Matthew 19:26).

We saw in the last chapter that effective prayer flows from humility and is fuelled by faith, and we have learned from Elijah that such faith thrives on apparent trivia and insignificance. But to humility and faith we must now add perseverance, learning to pray without respite until the rain comes and breakthrough finally appears. This is what it means to prevail in prayer.

Prevailing in prayer

Duncan Campbell sat in the pulpit at a large Christian conference in Bangor, Northern Ireland, where he was the main speaker. Something began to stir in his spirit and he sensed an almost irresistible compulsion to leave the convention and fly to the tiny Hebridean island of Bernera.

The inhabitants of Bernera numbered only about five hundred, less than the number attending the conference, and had been untouched by the recent revival on the larger islands nearby. But the compulsion in Campbell was too strong to ignore. He turned to the conference chairman and asked if he might be released to leave. The chairman refused, saying that he could not possibly excuse Campbell from delivering the final address. But Campbell pointed out that God was unlikely to anoint the sermon if he was calling him elsewhere, and the chairman reluctantly agreed.

Campbell flew from Ireland to Glasgow, and from there to Stornaway, capital of the Hebrides. From there he drove many miles north, finally crossing the waters to Bernera on the small ferry. At no point on the journey did he discuss his mission or reveal his identity to a single soul.

Stepping ashore at Bernera he approached a boy and asked where the nearest minister lived. The boy replied that both of the island's churches were without ministers at that time.

"Where then does the nearest church elder live?" Campbell inquired.

"In the house on the top of the hill", indicated the lad.

Campbell asked him to go and inform the elder that "Mr. Campbell" has come to the island, "and if he asks 'which Campbell' tell him 'the Campbell who was on Lewis.'"

The boy soon returned, out of breath, and even Campbell was startled by his reply: "Mr. MacKinnen has been expecting you. He has arranged for you to stay with his brother, and you are preaching in the church tonight."

A few days earlier, as Campbell sat in that pulpit in Bangor, Hector MacKinnen, the island postman had taken time off work to pray. He had become so disturbed by the spiritual ambivalence of his community that he committed the day to prayer in his barn. His wife recalled overhearing him pray for Duncan Campbell: "Oh God, I do not know where he is, but you know and I ask you to send him."

Breakthrough

At 10 p.m. that evening, MacKinnen "broke through"; that is, he received a sudden and certain conviction that his prayers had been answered. So sure was he that Campbell was coming upon the day in question that he arranged accommodation and notified the community that Mr. Campbell would be preaching the following Thursday at 9 p.m.!

Eighty people came to hear the visiting preacher that night, but nothing unusual happened. So ordinary was the meeting that Campbell even wondered whether he had mistaken God's call and should really have been preaching to the large numbers back in Bangor. But God was not responding to the faith of the renowned revival leader, but to that of a humble village postman who had received certainty from him in prayer.

The congregation left the building to make their way home, down the hill to the village below. MacKinnen approached Campbell and sitting beside him said, "Mr. Campbell, I hope you are not disappointed that revival has not come to the church tonight, but God is hovering over us and he will break through at any minute." Suddenly he stopped short, stood up and slowly removed his hat. Gazing intently into the night he whispered, "Stand Mr. Campbell, for God has come. See what is happening."

There below them on the hillside people were kneeling in the heather as loud cries of repentance began to fill the night air. The meeting, which had begun at 9 p.m. in the church continued until four in the morning on the hillside. The whole community was gripped by a "mighty visitation that shook the island from centre to circumference" and every single household was impacted that very night.

Praying until breakthrough

> *Therefore I tell you, whatever you ask for in prayer, believe that you have received it, and it will be yours* (Mark 11:24).

Hector MacKinnen was not someone who just "said prayers", nor was he simply a person with a disciplined prayer life; he knew *how* to pray. Much of our praying today is ineffective because we have not learned how to pray. One day the disciples approached Jesus and asked to be taught to pray. In response he gave them what is commonly known as "The Lord's Prayer", saying *This then is how you should pray: "Our Father..."* (Matthew 6:9).

Please note that Jesus doesn't say "this is *what* you should pray." The Lord's prayer is first and foremost a model of how to pray and not a script for repetition. In fact, Jesus teaches that our words aren't actually that important, because God listens to the heart — not our *babbling... many words* (Matthew 6:7), and he responds to our faith, not our phraseology.

Hector MacKinnen had learned to pray in faith, which is why he persevered all day until breakthrough came. As he knelt in that barn and asked God to send Duncan Campbell, he reached a moment of assurance, in which he knew that he had been heard (Mark 11:24). That is why he could confidently book the church and arrange accommodation. Faith perseveres and does not relent until the answer comes. I wonder how much of our praying stops short of breakthrough? We must learn the lesson Hudson Taylor scribbled in his diary one night on Brighton beach: "To move man, through God, by prayer alone."[49]

Persevering in prayer

Most revival accounts make reference to this experience of "prevailing" in prayer, continuing until "One becomes actually aware of receiving, by firmest anticipation, and in advance of the event, the thing for which one asks."[50] Having received a sense of breakthrough it then seems pointless to pray any more because the intercessor knows with certainty that God has heard and acted. Charles Finney gives a remarkable example of such prevailing prayer:

> *The first ray of light that broke in upon the midnight which rested on the churches in Oneida County, in the fall of 1825, was from a woman in feeble health who, I believe, had never been in a powerful revival. Her soul was exercised about sinners. She was in agony for the land. She did not know what ailed her, but she kept praying more and more, till it seemed as if her agony would destroy her body. At length she became full of joy, and exclaimed 'God has come! God has come! There is no mistake about it, the work is begun and is going on all over the region.' And sure enough, the work began and her family were almost all converted, and the work spread over that part of the country. Now do you think that woman was deceived? I tell you, no. She knew she had prevailed with God in prayer. She had travailed in birth for souls, and she knew it.*[51]

On one occasion during the Hebridean awakening, Duncan Campbell was praying in a part of the island as yet untouched by the movement, locked away in the local minister's study. The minister was out in the field when he was startled by a shout. Turning, he saw Campbell running towards him calling out, "It's coming! It's coming! We've got through at last! We are over the top!" And sure enough, the revival broke through in that community that very night.

Although such experiences of prevailing in prayer mark out most revivals, they should not be seen as essential to the answering of prayer. After all, when an angel released Peter from prison in answer to the church's prayers he found them still interceding for him when he presented himself at the house (Acts 12:12)! In this instance the intercessors were oblivious to the fact that their prayers had "broken through" so dramatically.

Waiting for the answer

The disciples *joined together constantly in prayer* (Acts 1:14) right up to the moment when the Spirit came at Pentecost. They remembered that Jesus had told them to remain in Jerusalem until the promised baptism with the Holy Spirit and because they loved and trusted him they obeyed. They didn't see themselves as super-heroes, they had no clue that they were about to become Bible characters or that they were on the verge of an explosion that would shake the earth. There was no heavenly wall-planner hanging in the upper room with angels pointing to the day of Pentecost. They were not able to count off the hours, "Bring your sandwiches on Thursday ladies because that's the big day!" They simply knew that Christ had spoken and that his word could be trusted no matter how long it took. So they just waited and prayed, without any other plans for the future, while their businesses suffered and worried family members expressed concern. What a challenge this is to our culture of the immediate and the speed with which we lose heart.

Jesus told the parable of the persistent widow to emphasise this very principle, *that they should always pray and not give up* (Luke 18:1-8). The disciples probably remembered and re-told it as they passed the long hours in the upper room, reeling from the trauma and the wonder of recent events and anticipating his promise of "another helper".

Daniel, we are told, would get down on his knees and pray three times a day. One day, as he read the book of Jeremiah, God showed him that the exile would come to an end after seventy years. Taking God at his word he turned to the Lord God and pleaded with him in prayer and petition, in fasting and in sackcloth and ashes (Daniel 9:3). Daniel humbled himself and took it upon himself to confess the sins of his nation, interceding for mercy and forgiveness. He prayed passionately and with perseverance because he believed the firm promise of God. Three weeks later we find Daniel still persevering in prayer, fasting meat, wine and even body lotion (Daniel 9:3)! Eventually an angel appears and tells him Since the first day that you set your mind to gain understanding and to humble yourself before your God, your words were heard, and I have come in response to them. But the prince of the Persian kingdom resisted me twenty-one days (Daniel 10:12-13).

Spiritual warfare

Here we have a glimpse of the spiritual dimension that explains the need for persistence in prayer. It is not that God is slow to act, or that we are trying to persuade God (for prayer is laying hold of his highest willingness). Prayer requires persistence because it is also an act of warfare against the spiritual forces of evil in the heavenly realms (Ephesians 6:12). Such prayer reverses the Fall in which Adam asserted his independence. In it we say "not my will, but yours be done." We fight on God's side to liberate enemy-occupied territory, knowing that while the victory is certain, the length of the battle is not. Finney once bellowed: "Let hell boil over and spew out as many demons as there are stones in the pavement. If it causes Christians to draw close to God in prayer, the demons can't hinder a revival."[52]

Prayer warriors

Because we are caught up in a battle between opposing kingdoms, we have no choice but to fight. Ed Silvoso, an Argentinean church leader now based in California, led a workshop in Manila in 1989 about the importance of spiritual warfare in the Argentinean awakening. There he said: "If there is one dominant element that has emerged in the theology and methodology of evangelism in Argentina, I would say it is spiritual warfare. It is an awareness that the struggle is not against a political or a social system. Nor is it on behalf of those who are captives, but it is rather against the jail keepers, against the rulers, those in authority in the spiritual realm."[53]

At times such warfare will cost us everything. Jesus sweated blood as he entered the greatest battle ever fought. Paul was able to wish himself separated from Christ for the sake of others. James is said to have been called "old camel knees" because of the calluses he grew from kneeling so much in prayer.

A couple of years ago I was asked to run the youth programme at a large Christian event. A meeting had just finished and young people were rushing around, skateboarding and chatting. Someone came to me very concerned about two girls who were sobbing uncontrollably and almost screaming in the corner. I asked a responsible woman to go and sort it out and watched as she talked to the girls. Soon, she too broke down in tears and began crying out! Slightly annoyed at such immaturity on the part of my team member I went over myself. However as I got close enough to discern their words, I stopped in my tracks. These girls were not hysterical, they were crying out to God for a friend who was lost. So great was their burden in prayer that their hearts were breaking before his throne. They continued to pray like this for at least an hour and God heard their prayers. Such compassion in prayer challenged me profoundly.

Charles Finney tells of a prayer warrior with an even greater burden for the lost: "He prayed as if he would wreak violence on heaven. Blessings came so plainly in answer to his prayers that no one could doubt it. Should I tell you how he died? He prayed more and more, putting a map of the world in front of him. He looked over the countries and prayed for them until he died praying in his room. Blessed man! He was a prevailing prince of prayer."[54]

Birth Pains

During the revival on Lewis, many of the greatest intercessors were women. Their prayers were passionate and persistent so that they generally missed the meetings because they were elsewhere praying. One lady described these unusual prayer gatherings: "The breath of the Spirit would come and it was like women being in childbirth. We would fill up and fill up and fill up with the breath of God, and we would be in agony, and suddenly there would be relief as the new soul was born. Then the weight would come again and we would fill up again and again and others would be born into the Kingdom."[55]

Of course, Paul himself describes the groans of creation as "the pains of childbirth" which echo the Spirit's heart rending intercession for us *with groans that words cannot express* (Romans 8:26). Finney's account of the prayer warrior of Oneida County describes a similar experience: "She was in agony... but she kept praying more and more, till it seemed as if her agony would destroy her body. At length she became full of joy, and exclaimed, 'God has come!' She had travailed in birth for souls, and she knew it."

The intercessory prayer associated with revival has been compared to childbirth surprisingly often. Frank Bartleman, who was one of the intercessors of the Azusa Street outpouring, picked up the familiar refrain in his diary: "At Smale's church one day, I was groaning at the altar. The spirit of intercession was upon me. A brother rebuked me severely. He did not understand it. The flesh naturally shrinks from such ordeals. The 'groans' are no more popular in most churches than is a woman in birth-pangs in the home. Soul travail does not make pleasant company for selfish worldlings. But we cannot have souls born without it. Childbearing is anything but a popular exercise, and so with a real revival of new born souls in the churches… Men run from the groans of a woman in travail of birth. And so the church desires no 'groans' today. She is too busy enjoying herself."[56]

Such intercessors have learned what it means to prevail in prayer, persevering through the day of small things to lay hold unrelentingly of God's promises. As did Elijah, so have they heard the sound of a heavy rain and seen the dark clouds gathering, far beyond the horizon of human sight.

CHAPTER 10

PRAYER KEY 3: STANDING IN THE GAP

I looked for a man among them who would… stand before me in the gap on behalf of the land so that I would not have to destroy it, but I found none.

Ezekiel 22:10

Intercessory prayer

The Old Testament priesthood attempted to bridge the gap between God and humanity using gory sin-sacrifices. Ordinary, sinful people knew that if they brought their sacrificial offering to the temple, a priest would offer it up to God and minister his grace to them in return. Many great biblical heroes modelled this intermediary, priestly role bridging the gap between God and his people, from Moses and Joshua to David and Nehemiah.

The New Testament teaches that Jesus is the ultimate High Priest bridging the gap between us and the Father through the cross, and interceding perpetually on our behalf (Romans 8:26-34, Hebrews 7:25). As those who are "in Christ Jesus" and "ministers of his grace", the church takes on this priestly role, as the body of the Great High Priest. The ministry of every Christian therefore, is essentially intercessory: to present the world to God (1 Peter 2:5) and God to the world (1 Peter 2:9):

- Presenting the world to God involves worship, sacrifice and prayer.
- Presenting God to the world is prophetic and evangelistic: proclaiming the wonders we have seen and heard to all the earth.

Intercession, therefore, may be seen as the joining of prayer and prophecy: "As… a mediatorial service that declares the will of God to human-kind and bears human need before God's throne in prayer."[57]

Identifying with sin

The Word became flesh (John 1:14). These four words are arguably the most astounding in the Bible. It is stupefying that the eternal Word, who was "with God in the beginning" and through whom "all things were made", should choose to become human. But Jesus knew that, in order to become our Great High Priest and bridge the sin-gap that divorces us from God, he would have to become flesh. It was not enough for him to remain at the right hand of the Father to plead on our behalf, he had to become his prayers. By the same principle, as we intercede for individuals, communities and nations, we too will have to identify with them and even be willing to bear their sins and wounds.

Like many churches we have planted a number of new congregations over recent years. But one of the things that often surprises people is the fact that when we do so every member of the planting team will move house into the new community. This can have quite an impact on local estate agents, schools and curry houses, but such identification is vital to the success of the new church. It shows that we are not just driving in from afar for a weekly meeting, but that we are deeply committed to the community itself. It is the model of incarnation, an intercessory act of identification with lost souls and people groups. And so, for instance, if there is bullying in the local school, it becomes a concern we share first hand because it now threatens our children too; if there is crime on the streets it now affects us. Equally, we discover and benefit from the good, positive aspects of the new environment. Our prayers, and indeed our lives, now flow from personal experience rather than distant concern.

Intercessory prayer can only really flow out of a deep level of personal identification. Compare the way we pray for a starving child in Africa to the way we would pray for our own child. The difference is not so much the scale of emotion as the level of intimacy. When distant strangers become intimate neighbours our prayers for them find passion. The Bible is full of such identification. Jeremiah identified so strongly with Israel's pain that he wrote: *Oh my anguish, my anguish! I writhe in pain. Oh, the agony of my heart… the whole land lies in ruins* (Jeremiah 4:19). Hosea was even called to identify with Israel's unfaithfulness to the extent of marrying an adulterous wife. When Nehemiah heard about the disgrace of Israel, *I sat down and wept. For some days I mourned and fasted and prayed before the God of heaven. Then I said: "O Lord… I confess the sins we Israelites, including myself and my father's house, have committed against you."* (Nehemiah 1:4-6)

Sins of the nation

As we seek God for national revival, we have a priestly duty to confess the sins of our nation. In Scripture this is never a detached theological exercise, but a heart-cry, often accompanied by fasting, mourning and the wearing of sackcloth and ashes. In such prayer, we acknowledge that the filth of society infects and affects us too, and we cry out that in God's perfect anger, he would remember mercy and spare us. Daniel prayed a remarkable intercessory prayer for Israel, owning its disobedience as his own, although he himself was "highly esteemed" by God (Daniel 10:11). *While I was speaking and praying, confessing my sin and the sin of my people Israel and making my request to the Lord my God for his holy hill… Gabriel came to me in swift flight* (Daniel 9:21).[58]

Sins of the church

Sadly, we must also own the sins of the church since no one part of the body can detach itself from the rest and claim purity. The terrible truth is that Christ's body is riddled with sickness. There is institutional inflexibility, disregard for scripture, a quenching of the Spirit, gross materialism, sexual immorality and division. No local expression can ignore the bigger problems, nor can any denomination, network or group achieve theological purity and holiness by separation or cutting itself off. Unity means loving one another enough to appreciate our differences, share our successes, and eve carry the shame of each other's sin.

Unity

Charles Finney said that the two prerequisites for revival are prayer and unity. Without a commitment to work with other churches and bless other traditions, we cannot expect our prayers for revival to be heard. Unity must be our top priority, therefore, for at least three major reasons: God commands it, revival requires it, and it is good for our health!

God commands unity

Remarkably, Jesus only ever commanded us to do two things: preach the Gospel (Matthew 28:20) and love one another (John 13:34). It is the depth of our love for each other, not our doctrinal purity, that marks us out as Christians. Jesus' final prayer for the church was that all of them may be one… so that the world may believe that you have sent me (John 17:20-21). I suspect he knew that Satan's strategy against us down the years would be to divide and conquer. He definitely knew that God bestows blessing wherever brothers live together in unity (Psalm 133:1).

Revival requires unity

The revival in Argentina is one of the longest and most documented in the history of the modern church. Its leaders, like Finney, place the issues of prayer (particularly spiritual warfare) and of church unity right at the heart of their model. Ed Silvoso, for example, lists unity as the primary step in "preparing an atmosphere for effective evangelism".[59] As we pray for revival, therefore, it is essential that we allow God to convict us of any trace of competitiveness, jealousy or sectarian prejudice against other flavours of sincere Christian faith.

Unity is good for your health!

Unity does not require uniformity and it is actually a good thing that the …h is made up of so many different denominations, streams and … How sad it would be if we had to worship like clones, when … all so different! The unity that commands God's … lves loving — and liking — one another. We … doctrine and I suspect God doesn't want us to all believe exactly the same things about everything anyway! Wesley, Whitefield and Edwards are excellent role models for us in this. They worked together wholeheartedly, spoke well of each other unreservedly and agreed to disagree on points of theology and practice. Fellowship with those who think differently is good for us, just as cross pollination is always healthier than inbreeding.

The prayer that prepares the way of the Lord goes far deeper than saying "please send revival" in a thousand different ways. It is moved by passion for the church and compassion for the lost. It identifies with the wounds and the sins of others and it wrestles, like Jacob, with God for the blessing (Genesis 32:22-32). From that moment onwards his identity was utterly, perhaps terrifyingly, caught up in the promise of God for a nation. We too should embrace the name, the identity and the destiny of our communities. But priestly identification at such a level can cost a very great deal; having wrestled with God, Jacob limped for the rest of his life.

Praying the price

Prayer warriors will often carry scars that are righteous trophies of battle, the wounds of the faithful. I'm not talking about hurts and insecurities, which relate to the selfishness of others and need to be healed. I'm talking about the intercessory pain and anguish often experienced prior to breakthrough. The enemy will often target intercessors as they lead God's people into battle, and although they know the joy of breakthrough, they may also carry the scars of the fight.

Moving house is never easy. Lorraine Fenner, who coordinates our church's intercession ministry, has successfully prayed a number of people into houses that they had been struggling to buy. It is as though her prayers can cut through interminable legal red tape. But ironically, Lorraine's own family lived in cramped conditions for a number of years, unable to move as potential houses fell through at the last moment with depressing regularity. There are numerous accounts of revival leaders with remarkable ministries whose private lives were riddled with personal suffering. The apostle Paul experienced such frustration on an even bigger scale. Having been used to perform remarkable miracles, he lived his life with a "thorn in the flesh" that God would not remove.

It is no coincidence that many prayer warriors have known a great deal of personal pain, and this has somehow refined their faith and focused their eyes on eternity in a way that makes Satan tremble. Such prayer warriors should be honoured and protected by the church because their ministry is probably the most sacrificial service Christians can give themselves to. That is why the church thrives on the blood of martyrs: martyrdom is the ultimate sacrifice, unlocking the purest power of the cross.

The price paid by those in revival is little compared to that of those who prayed it in, and I suspect that particular honour awaits these faithful forerunners in heaven. "It may be that in the eyes of God it is a greater honour to be chosen prior to the outbreak of revival, to be an emissary and a channel of the living God in the preparation time, in the harder time, than in revival time itself. Masses of people then will benefit from the flooding of the rivers of God, but the honour of the battlefield, I suggest, is given to the pioneers who prepare the way for the later flood tides. It may be that you now live in the hour of greatest opportunity from God's standpoint. What an hour in which to be alive!"[60]

III: PREPARING THE CHURCH

Oh, that God would make us dangerous!

Jim Elliot

Living according to Kingdom values requires Christians to place relationships higher than personal freedom.

Ralph Neighbour

CHAPTER 11

STARTING AN EPIDEMIC

The third millennium probably sneaked in surreptitiously during 1996, as unnoticed as the birth that began it all in a stable two thousand years before. But while historians squabble over the precise date of Jesus' birth there is no question that his life and death have had an incalculable impact upon world history. As a result there are about 1.8 billion Christians alive today. During the twentieth century alone more than six billion copies of the New Testament have been sold, with its text translated into two thousand languages and dialects. This is fame on a massive scale.

Writing in the *Daily Telegraph*, Paul Johnson described the Gospels as "the very building blocks of our civilisation. Without them… Giotto would not have painted his frescoes at Arena; Dante would not have written the *Divine Comedy*; Mozart would not have composed his *Requiem* and Wren would not have built St. Paul's Cathedral."[61]

But how did Jesus achieve all this? He never wrote a book; he never started a Bible School; he didn't enter politics or resort to military might; he rarely left his insignificant homeland; he had no influential friends to mention; he didn't begin a dynasty or leave a will; he had no formal training and no money. Perhaps most bewildering of all, his ministry spanned little more than one thousand days and yet its impact has snowballed for two thousand years. So how is such influence possible?

Jesus' formula was disconcertingly simple: he started this two thousand year epidemic by "infecting" just a handful of ordinary people with his wonderful, contagious presence, and it was through them that the "virus" spread from Jerusalem to the ends of the earth. Tradition suggests that Thomas travelled as far as India, spreading the Gospel in his wake.

The epidemic of revival

In 1997 international headlines reported the potential epidemic that threatened to decimate Hong Kong. Although "bird flu" had actually killed only twenty people, the terrifying potential for destruction was projected at twenty per cent of the population of over six million, The Hong Kong Government spent millions of dollars incinerating chickens, which were known to be carrying the disease.

In situations such as these, statisticians use certain mathematical formulae to predict the extent of the impending epidemic. They have discovered that the two most critical determining factors are:

1. The intensity of the initial infection (i.e. how virulent the disease is).
2. The number of meaningful contacts the original carrier has. Thus, for instance, an infected pensioner who lives alone is far less likely to start an epidemic than a student living in halls of residence.

John Hayward, of the Department of Mathematics and Computing at the University of Glamorgan, developed the novel idea of applying these principles to revival and his conclusions are remarkable.[62] Hayward suggests that revival is constrained by the same two factors as an epidemic. First there has to be an intensity of initial infection (an unusually strong passion for Jesus) and second the infected carriers (Christians) require an extensive network of meaningful relationships with non-carriers.

If the genesis and extent of revival can indeed be projected along similar lines to an epidemic, there are dramatic lessons to be learned

Intensity of infection

Every revival begins with a small but significant number of people who become "infected" with fresh excitement about the Lord. It appears to be necessary, therefore, to create contagious environments for this to take place, in which God's powerful presence can be experienced over a protracted period of time. Revivals begin in meetings. The exact content of such meetings will vary from community to community, but will always involve prayer, waiting on God and probably some form of ministry. There is evidence historically that such gatherings and waiting periods can indeed serve to infect people in such a way that their faith becomes dynamically contagious.

Prior to Pentecost the believers gathered together "constantly in prayer" while Peter expounded the scriptures. There must have been an amazing sense of significance and destiny as they discovered that their (previously inconsequential) lives now appeared to be intertwined with ancient biblical prophecy. King David himself, Peter pointed out, predicted Judas' tragic suicide (Acts 1:16). They probably never tired of telling their personal stories of the resurrected Jesus: what he had said, how he had looked, and with one hundred and twenty of them packed in that upper room it is easy to imagine their anticipation. Such an environment cultured in them an infection so contagious that when the Spirit's power finally fell at Pentecost, there could be no stopping its spread.

The practical implication is that we need to apply our creative resources to the task of gathering Christians in such environments once again. The reality is that most Christians attending meetings are not gospel carriers. They return to their daily routine unaffected and as a result, no matter how much they are exhorted to evangelise, they are unlikely to do so with any measure of success. After all, it is impossible to pass on an illness that you are not yourself carrying. At the time of writing, Gerald Coates is gathering Christians at Marsham Street in Westminster, London to "sow the seeds of revival". Thousands have passed through the doors to pray and wait on God for awakening. The meetings have attracted extensive media coverage, ironically more from the secular media than the Christian press, which begs the observation that society at large might currently have more faith for revival than the British church.

Gathering points such as this, not to mention the global ministry of Toronto Airport Christian Fellowship and events such as Spring Harvest and Soul Survivor, undoubtedly stir the faith of the church and could quite easily become epicentres for revival.

If revival does indeed proceed along the same exponential lines as an epidemic, two other points made by John Hayward are encouraging to note. First, that revival can start with just a few people. God doesn't necessarily need hundreds of people to start a revival. In fact the tiniest group could actually begin an enormous awakening. If anything, the statistics suggest that although the initial growth from a small group will be slower, the ensuing revival is likely to last longer than one that begins with a large number of carriers. We see this in situations like the Hebridean awakening where one small prayer meeting went on to achieve such disproportionate results.

The second point is that revival might already have begun! Large scale revivals aren't necessarily obvious for the first few years, until they reach a certain critical mass.[63] If a national church amounting to ten per cent of the population were to grow to sixteen per cent in just fifteen years, only one sixth of that increase would occur in the first five years, and such growth might appear fairly unremarkable. The bulk of the growth would come in the following seven years, and this would be the time when it became broadly evident that something extraordinary was taking place. The Great Awakening is a good example of this because, although it began in 1739, most people in England were oblivious to the fact that anything unusual was happening until the middle of the century. And the real impact in terms of church growth came in the latter half of the century. It is perfectly possible, therefore, that God has already begun a reviving work in the nation, but that it is not yet obvious beyond certain pockets.

A drug-dealing hippie came to Christ a few years ago and lived with me and my wife for three years. A cocktail of drug abuse had left him hurting and paranoid. In fact he was so afraid of being used that for a while he refused to stroke the cat in case it was just manipulating him with its purring and pretended affection! On one occasion he found himself so intimidated by a group of students that he quietly climbed into a cupboard and hid. It took Paul a long time before he felt able to receive Christ's unconditional love for himself, but as he did so he found healing and freedom and has become a truly whole person, with a deep desire to care for others.

Paul visited the Pensacola revival in the summer of 1997, and having spent a week in that contagious environment came back seriously infected. A few days later he started a course in social work at university and was asked to say a little bit about himself to the other students on his course. Now everybody else had simply introduced their name and given a short explanation of why they wanted to become social workers, but Paul was carrying something he could not keep to himself. He started by giving his name (no problems so far). Next Paul explained that he had recently moved to Portsmouth in order to help start a new church (a few raised eyebrows). Then, surrounded by politically-correct humanists, Paul announced that he wanted to become a social worker because God had rescued him from living hell and he wanted to be able to do for others what Jesus Christ had done for him.

Paul assumed that everyone would write him off as the religious fanatic of the class, but during the coffee break he found himself surrounded by inquisitive people desperate to know more about his story. They couldn't equate such passionate Christian faith with his long, matted hair and outrageous clothing. So Paul agreed to tell his remarkable story. While he was still speaking, one of the listeners began to tremble and left the group in search of a chair. When Paul found her later she told him that she had felt a power in his words making her shake and that she would have fallen over had she not removed herself from earshot. She was concerned to know what was behind this experience and Paul explained that God loved her and was trying to touch her life. "Is there anything I can read about this?" she stammered. Paul suggested she try the Bible.

Here we see the power of God's infection, passing contagiously from Pensacola to Paul and through him to a network of friends. So we must now turn our attention to the second regulating factor: the number of meaningful contacts that infected Christians have with non Christians. After all, if the enemy cannot vaccinate the church against the gospel virus itself, he will at least endeavour to quarantine the virus-carriers in holy huddles, and thus limit the spread.

Meaningful contacts

A few years ago I determined to discover the source of our church's evangelistic growth and was surprised to find that it was not coming from our evangelism, by which I mean our street theatre team, our door to door visitation programme, our "Parties with a Purpose" and our "Just Looking" courses. These things, for all their possible merits, were effectively barren; the occasional person who did make a commitment through any of these channels generally fell away, if ever they made it to church in the first place.

So where was our increase coming from? I discovered that almost all of our evangelistic growth was the fruit of a remarkably small number of individuals. Most of them were not perceived as traditional evangelists, and a few were positively marginal to the church. But these people had two things in common: they were passionate about God and they had extensive contact with non-Christians. I now realise that they were, unwittingly, carrying the revival code; combining gospel-infection with friendship-evangelism.

I have a theory that the sparks of revival fall on a fairly regular basis in many Christian gatherings but that because few meaningful non Christian networks are represented, there is no tinder for these sparks to ignite, and so the intended blaze never even spreads beyond the meeting. A Californian church census discovered that seventy-one per cent of those converted do so as a result of a friend or relation. This is consistent both with the New Testament model of evangelism which was primarily person to person, and also with John Hayward's epidemic thesis. It means that the parts of society most likely to experience revival are those with a strong sense of community, where there is a great deal of meaningful, interpersonal contact, such as schools, university campuses, prisons or the close-knit gypsy networks. It also means that working class culture is more receptive to a mass movement of God than the highly individualistic middle and upper classes with their selective dinner parties, rarefied office environments and personal space. Significantly, this list of cultures reflects Christ's own priorities towards children, prisoners, the poor and dispossessed. Perhaps it is no coincidence that various gypsy and prison communities are experiencing revival even as I write.

The church may well need to repent for having absorbed the middle class cult of personal privacy (even at times arguing a theology for it), when this is such a hindrance to the spread of the gospel. After all, Jesus clearly lived his life in public, sharing even his most intimate moments with others. This was his strategy for discipleship, and remains the only one that works. It is certainly true in my experience that those people I have discipled most effectively have been the ones I have shared the most of my life with. George Whitefield was once asked if a particular man was a Christian; his telling reply was "I don't know, I've never lived with him." Whitefield clearly understood that authentic Christianity is expressed in daily (rather than weekly) fellowship.

This is not to say that personal space is unimportant. Jesus would often get up early and remove himself from the gaze of others in order to pray and be alone with his Father. But note the priorities: Jesus was normally with others, but he would occasionally remove himself to find privacy. However we have reversed this and tend to live as much of our lives as possible in private, at home, closeted away from unwanted intrusion, occasionally removing ourselves to spend time with others.

Diary culture

The middle classes have exalted the engagement diary to previously unimaginable heights of grandeur. It has been renamed "Personal Organiser" or even "Time Management System" and repackaged to twice the size of an ordinary Bible. Diaries in themselves are useful things and there is no spiritual premium in forgetting appointments or being disorganised. But the danger is that we can use a diary like a drawbridge which determines when we step out of our castles to "go to church" or "go to work" or when we invite selected people across the threshold to dinner, or perhaps a weekly meeting. When revival comes it will not bow to our schedules but will intrude upon our privacy. Like fire, a move of God's Spirit cannot be contained, regulated or tidied up. But despite this fact, most Christians choose to seclude themselves as much as possible, reducing the potential for the spread of revival.

This over-emphasis on private lives and personal space is contrary to the example of the early church, who gathered together constantly. We read that they would meet daily, after work, in one another's homes and in the temple courts or at Solomon's Colonnade. They were together all the time, and doubtless when they felt the need of a little solitude they would follow Jesus' example and get up early. To be a Christian was to live your life with others, under the public scrutiny of daily fellowship. As a result, there must have been little scope for hypocrisy among believers, and the Jerusalem church was highly visible and easily accessible to outsiders. In stark contrast, the most visible and accessible thing about most modern churches is an ancient building that stands empty all week while its members go about their "real" lives.

This principle of communal living continued throughout the first three centuries. It is thought that one of the sociological keys to the bewildering growth of the church throughout the Roman world was the predominance of urban *insulae*, densely packed apartment blocks in which there was a very high level of interchange between neighbours. The entire population of such a complex would soon be speculating when they saw the family on the fourth floor carrying their household gods down the long flight of stairs to discard with the rubbish. Rumours would spread about their new-found supernatural powers, and there is evidence that Christians would often be called in by non-Christian neighbours to conduct exorcism or healing.[64]

Church gets privatised

Sadly, by the beginning of the Middle Ages this radical model of church as true community had fundamentally changed. Church had now come to be associated with an institution in which the laity became passive observers, and the sense of community had all but gone. This resulted in an individualistic approach to spirituality that has been profoundly damaging to the mission of the church ever since. Richard F. Lovelace compares this misconception of personal faith (in which the lone believer receives grace primarily through isolated interaction with God) to a deep-sea diver drawing his oxygen from the surface through a hose. "He is essentially a self-contained system cut off from the other divers working around him. If their air supply is cut off, this does not damage him nor can he share with them the air that he receives. The situation would be no different if he were working alone a hundred miles away."[65]

Lovelace goes on to emphasise the sad implications of such individualism: "The normal Christian life is not simply a function of an individual believer's relationship to God. If he is isolated from Christians around him who are designed to be part of the system through which he receives grace, or if those Christians are themselves spiritually weak, he cannot be as strong and as filled with the Spirit as he otherwise would be." The remarkable truth is that our environment can actually limit the extent to which we are Spirit-filled, which brings us back to the two prerequisites of revival: the need for a contagious environment and for meaningful fellowship.

The individualism of the mediaeval church was not really overcome by the Reformation. A passive collection of believers swapped the weekly act of observing a priest for the weekly act of listening to a preacher. But the church still lacked any real sense of community and as a result had little impact on its members — let alone on unbelievers.

With the Enlightenment and the rise of rationalism, the individual became the measure of all things. The metaphysical poet John Donne, who became a Christian, was a lone voice objecting that "no man is an island".

One of the most obvious outworkings of this individualistic heritage is the model of the insular, nuclear family that prevails throughout the western world today. This contrasts starkly with the extended families and interactive communities found throughout the rest of the world. Significantly, the Hebridean Islands are an exception to the Western norm, with a Gaelic model of extended family and tight-knit village life. The densely populated Welsh mining towns through which revival swept in 1904 were just the same, as are the gypsy networks and prison environments experiencing revival today. By contrast, there are people in my street who, to my shame, I can't even name; revival might break out three doors down, but there's no guarantee that I would even hear about it.

The challenge of de-privatising our faith — of sharing our lives rather than just having a succession of meetings with people — can strike right at the heart of our security. As I have preached this message I have often been amazed at the reaction it can provoke. Staunchly committed church members, who give money sacrificially and commit time to several meetings a week, can struggle with the deep implications of opening their homes and extending their commitment to family. We often say that church is not the meeting but the people, but perhaps we fail to practice what we preach when we fail to truly share our lives with one another. A church might be lively, with well attended meetings, without really practising Christian community at a meaningful level. Many churches do indeed maintain a deep level of fellowship and love and their Sundays are a wonderful expression of this. But for others Sunday brings a congregation of lonely individuals and self-sufficient family units who line up in pews or chairs, sing and drink coffee from plastic cups, but are relative strangers for the rest of the week. Members of such churches are rarely heard, scarcely known and isolated until their needs reach crisis point. The implications are devastating for our evangelism, discipleship and pastoral care. After all, it is by our love for one another that the world will know that we are disciples of Jesus and not just members of an obscure religious club. Every parent knows that family life demands more than Sunday and Wednesday nights, it requires your all. Is church really your new family, your place of rest, the context for your whole life as it was for the first disciples, or is it actually just a series of meetings that you attend, or even lead, as a committed member?

One church leader was profoundly challenged by this need to surrender even his privacy to God. He wrestled for a while, alone with his Lord, before taking out his front door keys, slapping them down on the table in front of him and saying "OK God, you can even have these". He and his wife with their new baby have now moved to a larger house so that they can extend their family with lodgers and a constant stream of visitors. At a stage of life when there is a very strong cultural pull upon young families to internalise, this remarkable couple are pioneering. There is a price to pay in opening your home, welcoming strangers and sacrificing time with the television to spend with others. But like having children the blessings outweigh the sacrifice a hundred-fold.

Paul moved in with us just weeks after we got married and stayed for three years. At times this was a pressure; I dreaded coming home to find the fridge ransacked or arriving exhausted after a long night of meetings to find him waiting up to request prayer. But the blessing is incomparably worth it because my wife and I have found a son and a brother in Paul who gives us continual pride and pleasure, and our marriage is certainly the stronger for the sacrifices involved.

The revival code

A few years ago, we made friends with some teenagers on a local estate. We would go and play football with them on "their" turf and after a while they did us the enormous favour of coming to our house. We discovered that a couple of them were aptly named Nick and Rob as valuables began to disappear during their visits. But it was worth it.

One day my wife and I left the house to walk to the church prayer meeting. Four of these lads swooped up on their (stolen) bicycles and asked where we were going.

"Oh, just the prayer meeting" I replied nonchalantly.

John reflected for a second and then pronounced, "We'll come".

I was suddenly terrified by the prospect of these lads attending our sad little gathering and began to panic.

"Y-you can't", I floundered, "it's boring!"

"Oh, we don't mind that."

"But it's not aimed at young people…"

"That's OK."

I was getting desperate; we would soon reach the venue. I would have to play my trump card: "But you're not even Christians. You aren't supposed to pray!" But by this time it was too late, and four delinquent teenagers strode into that prayer meeting with us.

The meeting was indeed a trifle boring (that is until our guests handcuffed the worship leader to a radiator while he was deep in prayer!) But the fact remains that non-Christians wanted to attend the least dynamic meeting our church was offering at that time. I could pretend that this was a little taste of revival: "Pagan criminals flock to pray". But the truth is that they wanted to come because we had simply taken time to become their friends, and sharing our lives apparently included the boring bits.

When Christians lay down their personal space, and commit themselves to interact with one another and with the lost, I believe that they begin to touch something of the revival code. The gospel remains the power of God for salvation, which means that it can spread today as dynamically as it ever did. But for it to do so we must allow it to infect our churches with fresh passion for Jesus and we must build meaningful friendships with those who need God's healing virus the most. Anyone for an epidemic?

CHAPTER 12

CELLS: A REVIVAL WINESKIN

Now, after more than three centuries, we can, if we will, change gears again. Our opportunity for a big step lies in opening the ministry to the ordinary Christian in much the same manner that our ancestors opened Bible reading to the ordinary Christian. To do this means, in one sense, the inauguration of a new Reformation while in another it means the logical completion of the earlier Reformation in which the implications of the position taken were neither fully understood nor loyally followed.

Elton Trueblood[66]

At 2:20 a.m. on 15th April, 1912, the White Star liner *Titanic* collided with an iceberg on her maiden voyage, plummeting to the icy depths of the North Atlantic with a loss of 1,523 lives out of 2,228 on board. The special commission set up to investigate the calamity discovered a chilling twist to the tragedy. Days earlier White Star had reduced the number of Titanic's lifeboats from sixty-four to twenty because they made the deck of the "unsinkable" ship "look cluttered". A purely cosmetic decision had sentenced hundreds of people to the most terrifying of deaths.[67]

Our world is obsessed with superficial appearance and it is all too easy to apply such values even to the church. Jesus rebuked the Pharisees for being like whitened tombs, gleaming clean on the outside but full of death within; we might compare them to the

Titanic — an aesthetically pleasing death trap. How often God's people preoccupy themselves with the veneer of church politics, while the lost proceed to hell. How tempting it can be to hide personal chaos behind a public face, merely keeping up appearances from Sunday to Sunday. How readily we sweep sin under the ornate carpets of church life.

Yet movements of God's Spirit in renewal and revival invariably expose such hypocrisy and disturb the neatness of church life. As a result, awakening always has its religious opponents and, in the words of Jesus, serves as *a sign that will be spoken against, so that the thoughts of many hearts will be revealed* (Luke 2:34).

When Martin Luther nailed his *Ninety-five Theses* to the door of the Castle Church in Wittenburg on 31st October 1517 he could not have imagined the reaction it would provoke. After all, the young monk was simply objecting to the theology of selling indulgences (the relics contained within the Castle Church alone were reckoned to earn pilgrims a remission of 1,902,202 years and 270 days!) But within a fortnight news of Luther's moderate objection had reached every university and religious centre in the land and in 1518 he was reprimanded by his own Augustinian order. In 1520 the Pope himself ordered Luther to recant and in 1521 he was both excommunicated and outlawed — quite an achievement!

John Wesley knew that revival and unpopularity go hand in hand. He was banned from Anglican pulpits and repeatedly accused of inciting that terrible crime, "enthusiasm". He was also stoned, mobbed, regularly punched so that blood spurted from his mouth, clubbed and once a drunken clergyman even tried to ride his horse through Wesley's crowd!

Jonathan Edwards was ultimately compelled to resign from the church in which he had ministered powerfully and selflessly throughout the New England revival.

When the power of God detonated the humble gathering at Azusa Street in 1906, there was unilateral derision from those offended by its apparently fanatical extremes: manifestations like tongues, shaking and falling to the ground and the improper fraternisation between blacks and whites. The power of God's presence was threatening to make a mess once again.

In our time, one of the common objections to the Toronto Blessing (though I am not equating this with revival) has been that it is "disorderly" and that God only ever generates order and propriety. Sadly such critics fail to see beyond the cultural offence of dramatic manifestations to the deep, internal workings of God's Spirit. They also ignore the fact that such manifestations have marked revivals of the past.[68]

The dynamic renewal leader David Watson memorably described this historic clash between orderliness and the reviving wind of God:

> *The wind of the Spirit blows with revival power, and for a time all is exciting, if a little unpredictable. However man comes along and tries to organise what is happening, because he wants to be in control. In fact he is frightened of not being in control. And the Holy Spirit sadly makes his departure. Sometimes I think of it as God opening the windows of the church. For a time there is a glorious fresh breeze and the stuffiness disappears. However, the breeze begins to blow some of the forms and papers all over the place; and with such unseemly confusion, church leaders firmly close the windows. The papers are once again arranged in the neat and orderly piles. But the windows are shut; the wind has gone, and the stuffiness returns.*[69]

Change is here to stay

How are we to ensure that when the winds of God's Spirit finally come we welcome him into our neat churches, resisting that perpetual urge to "firmly close the windows"?

The New Testament exhorts us to keep our church structures flexible, like the soft skin of a new wineskin that can expand to contain fermenting wine; or like a body that works to stay healthy, exercising to keep supple as the years go by. God's Spirit is always on the move; he is like breath, wind, a pillar of cloud or fire, a flowing river or a bird in flight. It stands to reason therefore that God fills churches that are willing to move, to change, to flow with him. In the wilderness years God required a portable tabernacle that could move whenever he did, unlike a static temple. There is a consistent call for fluid rather than institutional models of church, capable of reincarnation into a diversity of cultures and committed to perpetual reformation. One of the slogans of our church is that "change is here to stay", because we believe that God is always doing a new thing and his people are more often required to hoist sail than to drop anchor.

Cell church

Revival produces a host of wonderful problems. For instance, the world's largest churches in Seoul, Korea and Bogota, Colombia are far too big to ever meet together in a single venue. As a result members are only allowed to attend Sunday meetings in the church stadium once every few weeks! This has forced them to develop an effective cell structure where the primary expression of church is not the Sunday service but thousands of vibrant small-group communities.

Cell church is the predominant "wineskin" used in revival dynamics around the world and there is much that we can learn about this radical remodelling of church. Every member is encouraged to exercise ministry or priesthood in the context of a small discipling community (generally between six and fourteen people). Unlike house groups each cell has an evangelistic remit to multiply, and once it has grown sufficiently it will appoint another leader and divide in two. In accelerated revival scenarios such multiplication might take place every few weeks and a new Christian could easily be leading a group within a year of conversion!

Living cell groups become like epidemic centres, cultivating an intensity of infection as they absorb the presence of Jesus and grow together in faith. Significantly each group also represents a social network of non-Christian friendships through which Christ's contagious presence can easily spread. There is not enough space to even begin an adequate introduction to cell thinking in this book, but materials abound and I would particularly encourage readers to study William A. Beckham's *The Second Reformation*.[70]

But lest it be thought that cell-church is just some new formula or some fashionable trend, we should note that it is actually an entirely biblical way of building church and has been modelled since Pentecost.

Cells down the ages

When three thousand people were baptised on the day of Pentecost, they simply began to meet daily in one another's homes, breaking bread in the context of ordinary meals and dinner parties. This was the primary expression of fellowship and the main context for discipleship which was then also expressed in larger gatherings at Solomon's Colonnade or the Temple Courts. *Day after day, in the Temple Courts and from house to house, they never stopped teaching and proclaiming the good news that Jesus is the Christ* (Acts 5:42).

Throughout the first three centuries, Christians continued to gather in homes for worship, fellowship and discipleship. These small communities grew dramatically until by the third century there were at least six million Christians in the Roman Empire alone. Severe persecution had ensured that this growth was organic and almost invisible; there was little, if any, direct preaching to the masses because it was simply too dangerous. Instead the believers modelled the most remarkable, alternative lifestyles in the way that they loved one another, shared possessions and ministered to the sick. "Beauty of life," one of them contended, "...causes strangers to join our ranks... We do not talk about great things; we live them."[71]

With the "conversion" of Constantine and the institutionalisation of Christianity as a state religion, this cell dynamic became endangered. Beckham suggests that "by building cathedrals and placing rituals and leadership within those buildings, Constantine changed the very nature and life of the church as originally designed by Christ. The changes grew out of new ways of thinking about church as an organisation rather than an organism."[72]

However cell churches continued, particularly in the fledgling monastic movements amidst the desert fathers who refused to accept that the body of Christ could be institutionalised and politicised. From there, the great Celtic church planters continued to model dynamic, small church communities and in the sixteenth century even Martin Luther advocated a return to the values of cell church *ecclessiolae in ecclesia;* little churches within the church. "Those who want to be Christians in earnest," he wrote, "and who profess the gospel with hand and mouth should sign their names and meet alone in a house somewhere to pray, to read, to baptise, to receive the sacrament and to do other Christian works."[73] However, despite such good intentions, Luther never actually achieved such a dynamic and as a result the Reformation, for all its blessings, resulted in new institutions emerging rather than grassroots revival.

Sadly the Reformation ideal of the priesthood of all believers has never really been practised by Protestant or Catholic traditions which, to this day, build churches around a single professional leader. When churches only really recognise a single "priest" they limit themselves to a single expression of church, incomplete ministry and burnt-out leaders, unable to truly empower members to build church at a personal level day to day. I am convinced that this challenge of fundamentally remodelling church around the ministry of every member is one of the great Everests awaiting the Christian community in the twenty-first century.

The reason for Luther's "cell suggestion" probably lay in the fact that persecuted Anabaptists were modelling the community of Christ with an authenticity that unwittingly embarrassed the dry formalism of Luther's reforms. The radical Anabaptist tradition continued through movements such as the Mennonites and Count von Zinzendorf's ecumenical community at Herrnhut which indirectly triggered Britain's Great Awakening. Professor Lovelace comments: "The most deliberate and successful use of the small group principle in history… was the bond system of Count von Zinzendorf. The micro-community of Herrnhut [was] informed by an urgent sense of mission… It also suggests a paradigm for the transformation of the whole church."[74]

Wesley certainly adapted many of Zinzendorf's principles in developing the primitive Methodist "revival societies"; effectively a cell movement that gave rise to modern day Methodism. These societies were broken down into "classes" and "bands" which operated very much like a modern-day cell group. As Wesley travelled the nation, the establishment and development of these small groups was really his primary focus and he would train leaders and address the needs of local groups.

Today there are many expressions of cell thinking within a range of traditions. From the Roman Catholic Base Communities of Latin America and the Chinese "house" churches to the Protestant cell group movement they share a common desire to model the community of Christ around relationship, simple worship, easy access and service to the community around.

As we prepare the way of the Lord in our churches we will have to embrace change, to develop wineskins that can host the new wine of the coming revival. For if we will only pay the price of reform, there is every possibility that the next Great Awakening could last to usher in the end of the age. However, if our structures remain inflexible, unbiblical and impractical, God's precious new wine will come and go in a single season, unable to bless beyond a single generation. In this respect reformation and revival must walk hand in hand.

CHAPTER 13

CHURCH AND YOUTH CULTURE

It is high time we faced the fact that without a revolution in western youth culture there will be no awakening in our time.[75]

When he was President, George Bush paid a visit to an old people's home. After chatting to a number of the residents, he turned to an old lady and asked, "Do you know who I am?" "No," came the honest reply, "but if you ask at reception, I'm sure they will be able to help you."

Young people today are struggling to know their identity, but the vast majority of them are not finding it in Christ, and are evacuating churches faster than ever before. For instance, in the 1980s English churches managed to loose a staggering forty-nine per cent of their teenagers.[76] Exhaustive research shows that if we could merely hold on to the young people we have right now, the church nationally would be in a state of significant growth. And if we could actually attract new teenagers and students to the community of Christ, we would currently be experiencing growth equivalent to revival. Prayers for revival are, therefore, prayers for Generation X.

I was walking across a university campus at 2 a.m. as a night-club was emptying. A student with long hair and striking features caught up with me and, knowing that I was a Christian, challenged me to a conversation.

The "conversation" turned out to be more of a monologue as, for more than an hour, he enlightened me with his perspectives on Christianity, his frustrations with church and his desire to find a way of life reminiscent of Jesus. "I'm totally impressed with Jesus," he finally concluded, "but there's just nothing in Christianity or the church that attracts or inspires me." I searched his face for a trace of arrogance or cynicism and yet I found nothing but sadness in his eyes. I asked if he would help me build a church for people like him, and he agreed.

That young man's heart-cry is by no means unique; there is a common longing in the generation for spirituality and integrity without hierarchy and hypocrisy. That longing may at times be veiled in cynicism, but watch the crowd at a football match, a fan at a concert, or a young couple in love and you quickly see the God-given passion inherent in youth, which would gladly give its life for the hero of Calvary. But the challenge of mobilising such passion is enormous, as this generation seems more dissipated than any before.

Research reveals that after three minutes looking at pictures of models in magazines, seventy per cent of women feel "depressed, guilty and shameful". It seems that every girl is *supposed* to look like a supermodel, while only eight in the world *actually* do (and even they require airbrushing, plastic surgery and starvation diets to be worthy of the front page.)

More money is spent world-wide on advertising than on education, so it is now consumerism that educates us. One glossy arts magazine has the honesty to call itself *Dazed and Confused*, and the fruit of this confusion can be seen everywhere. For instance a recent advertising campaign for a unisex fragrance features supermodel Kate Moss preaching: "Be good, be bad, just be." This pseudo-philosophical garbage is attempting to sound cool, experimental and above all tolerant, but it is plainly ridiculous: drive an old lady over to the supermarket; drive over an old lady on the way home — it doesn't matter, "just be."

However, when presented with this bleak picture of today's youth culture it is worth remembering that every generation has despaired of its young. It was in 300 BC that Aristotle moaned: "When I look at the younger generation, I despair of the future of civilisation."

Young people and the purposes of God

In fact, young people have a remarkable spiritual pedigree and are to be found at the heart of every major move of God through history. The biblical words for youth (*naar* in Hebrew and *neanias* in Greek) are very positive, with connotations of heroism. This reflects the fact that throughout scripture we find God revealing a surprising propensity towards young people and children, consistently choosing the young and inexperienced over and above the mature and competent. It becomes very clear that God believes in the qualities of youth and that he has always used young people powerfully. For example:

- Joseph was just seventeen, with a whole host of glaring character faults, when he received his calling in the form of a dream (Genesis 37:2-11).
- Gideon was the youngest and least in his tribe; the most unlikely of choices to lead a national military uprising (Judges 6:15).
- David was the youngest of Jesse's sons, apparently the least eligible choice for Samuel's anointing (1 Samuel 19:1-13).
- Solomon was probably just twenty years old when the Lord appeared to him in a dream. Already king in place of his father David, he confessed, "I am only a little child and do not know how to carry out my duties", but when offered anything, he requested wisdom, which delighted God (1 Kings 3:7).
- An extreme example is God's calling of Jeremiah before his birth! No wonder he later reprimands the timid prophet for saying *I am only a child* (Jeremiah 1:4-10).
- Josiah was just eight years old when he became king. At the age of sixteen *while he was still young, he began to seek the God of his father David*... and then, when he was twenty, *he began to purge Judah and Jerusalem of high places*... (2 Chronicles 34:3-4).
- In the New Testament it is remarkable to discover that Mary would only have been around fifteen years old when she conceived and bore Jesus.
- Jesus himself at the age of twelve revealed remarkable understanding sufficient to amaze the religious leaders at the temple (Luke 2:41-52) and had completed his entire ministry by the youthful age of thirty-three.

- It is often forgotten that, at the stoning of Stephen, Saul (later Paul) was only *a young man* (Acts 7:58).
- Paul's son in the faith Timothy was also unconventionally young, called to lead people much older than him. As a result, Paul had to exhort him not to allow anyone to despise his youthfulness, but to be confident in God's calling. (1 Timothy 4:12)

No wonder Archbishop George Carey urges us to "remember that Christianity began as a youth mission. Jesus was a young man when he died and he gathered young people around him."[77] Church history continues to reveal this startling use of young people in the flow of God's Kingdom. For instance:

- John Calvin was converted at the age of twenty-five and within a year had completed the draft of his book *Institutes of the Christian Religion*, possibly the most influential theology book in church history.
- George Whitefield was just twenty-one when he began to preach and soon carried a higher profile than John Wesley, who was his senior.
- Dwight L Moody, the renowned American evangelist, planted a youth church in a vacant tavern in Chicago during the Awakening of the 1850s which became a launching pad for many remarkable ministries for the rest of that century.
- One account of the 1859 Welsh revival reports: "The youth of our congregations are nearly all the subjects of deep religious impressions. Very young people… children from ten to fourteen years of age, gather together to hold prayer meetings and pray very fervently… these sometimes prove instrumental in bringing the powerful influences of the revival to that particular locality. The majority of all the converts… are young people."
- Catherine Booth, who founded the Salvation Army with her husband William, had read the entire Bible eight times by the age of twelve. And by fourteen she had mastered Finney's *Systematic Theology*, the works of Wesley and many other classics, in spite of constant pain from curvature of the spine.
- God chose a twenty-six-year-old, Evan Roberts, to lead the Welsh Awakening of 1904 (which also began in a youth meeting

and in which the young played a primary role).
- Billy Graham's phenomenal global ministry was born in post-war youth rallies which attracted tens of thousands of teenagers and launched Youth for Christ.
- In Asia, the Chinese awakening is most extensive among young people, since more than half of that country's one billion population are under twenty years old.[78]

When Donald MacPhail received Christ at the age of sixteen in the full heat of the Hebridean awakening, it catapulted him into ministry. He carried something of the glory of God so powerfully that when a sailor returning on leave simply shook hands with him, the sailor felt the touch of God and was converted without a word being spoken.

MacPhail's greatest ministry was as a "front-line prayer warrior". Andrew Woolsey tells of an occasion when Duncan Campbell called on MacPhail only to find him on his knees in the barn with his Bible open. When interrupted by this great man, MacPhail was not flustered, nor did he jump to immediate attention. Instead he quietly said, "Excuse me a little, Mr Campbell, I'm having an audience with the King".

> *Some of the most violent outpourings of the Spirit during the revival came when he was asked to pray. In a police station in Barvas he stood up one night, simply clasped his hands together, and uttered one word — "Father". Everyone was melted to tears as the Presence of God invaded the house... But the most outstanding example of God's anointing upon him was in Bernera, a small island off the coast of Lewis. Duncan was assisting at a Communion season; the atmosphere was heavy and preaching difficult, so he sent to Barvas for some of the men to come and assist in prayer. They prayed, but the spiritual bondage persisted so much so that half way through his address Duncan stopped preaching. Just then he noticed this boy, visibly moved, under a deep burden for souls. He thought: "That boy is in touch with God and living nearer to the Saviour than I am." So, leaning over the pulpit he said: "Donald, will you lead us in prayer?"*
>
> *The lad rose to his feet and in his prayer made reference to the fourth chapter of Revelation, which he had been reading that morning: "O God I seem to be gazing through the open door. I see the Lamb in the midst of the Throne, with the keys of death and of hell at his girdle." He began to sob;*

then lifting his eyes towards heaven, cried: "O God, there is power there, let it loose!" With the force of a hurricane, the Spirit of God swept into the building and the floodgates of heaven opened. The church resembled a battlefield. On one side many were prostrated over the seats weeping and sighing; on the other side some were affected by throwing their arms in the air in a rigid posture. God had come.[79]

In the light of all these examples of God's commitment to the young, we must address the issue of the church's irrelevance to youth culture as a matter of supreme urgency. If we are to prime the church for the possibilities of the twenty-first century, we may well need to repent of our attitude towards young people and change our whole approach to youth ministry.

Church in youth culture

Looking at the spiritual needs of this generation it is easy to call for change, but harder to propose serious policies for addressing the problem. One of the few models proposing a practical way forward is the integrated youth church movement. In a number of locations congregations are being planted with the specific aim of reaching young people, respecting and redeeming their distinct cultures, rather than seeking to replace them. This movement springs out of the growing realisation that youth culture is now thoroughly post-Christian in its world-view and must be recognised and approached as a distinctive, pagan mission field. Research indicates that while sixty per cent of British young people today believe in God, the vast majority of them consider church entirely irrelevant to their lives.[80] This clearly challenges anyone with a heart for the lost to ask searching questions about how the church can change in order to embrace such a disillusioned generation.

The fact is that the Bible does not refer to our predominant model of youth groups but rather commissions us to develop discipling communities in every culture — which presumably includes youth. The shortcoming of the common-or-garden youth group is that it effectively baby-sits teenagers until they are considered old enough to [illegible] real members of the church. Consequently, the youth [illegible]st churches are not included in membership, nor are they encouraged to break bread, baptise, tithe or operate as true church. The Ephesians chapter four ministries of apostles, prophets, evangelists, pastors and teachers are not generally cultivated or recognised in youth, and the approach to discipleship tends to combine the occasional ice skating trip with weekly talks on how to merely survive as a Christian. This has obviously drifted a long way from the example of our youthful leader who gathered young people around him, entrusted them with the keys of the Kingdom, defied them to lay down their lives and commissioned them to take the nations as their inheritance. In most youth groups faithless shoe-gazing has replaced faith-filled horizon scanning. But by failing to resource young people adequately and to take sufficient risks with them we exacerbate and extend immaturity along cultural rather than biblical lines.

It is in response to this challenge that increasing numbers of churches are planting congregations with the express intention of reaching youth cultures and enabling young people to worship in their own ways. Amidst the struggles and challenges associated with all church planting and the particular pressures of being young, there are some wonderful models emerging, particularly in England. Many of these are attracting unchurched teenagers and exercising a profile and prophetic mantle disproportionate to their current size. A surprising number of television programmes have been made and magazine articles have abounded. New and refreshing expressions of worship have flowed from record decks, video screens and the full range of contemporary arts. Pete Ward, the Archbishop of Canterbury's Advisor for Youth Ministry, comments: "The aim of youth ministry should be to set free the cultural creativity of young people in worship. Youth culture has its own subcultural expressions of celebration, lamentation and community life. These indigenous cultural elements should become the building blocks for a new expression of worship and church life."[81]

Expressions of church in youth culture have provoked controversy, often being accused of splitting up the church family. Galatians 3:28 has been quoted repeatedly (and out of context, which actually refers to the equal rights of all Christians as firstborn sons): *There is neither Jew nor Greek, slave nor free.* These critics argue that youth churches separate old and young and so divide the body of Christ.

Traditional church leaders once accused John Wesley of the same thing; splitting the church by establishing his "Methodist classes" and thus "gathering churches out of churches." When asked if this accusation was fair, Wesley replied categorically: "If you mean only gathering people out of buildings called churches, it is. But if you mean, dividing Christians from Christians, and so destroying Christian fellowship, it is not."[82]

A cursory glance at most church meetings reveals a handful of young people sitting along the back row, entirely disengaged from the proceedings and yet somehow considered to be modelling Christian family! If those same young people were given their own context to worship and grow in faith, exercising leadership and socialising with the wider church in more culturally appropriate ways, surely that would be a far truer expression of their equal rights as first-born sons of God? Since we know that church consists of the relationships and not merely the meetings, the important thing is that young people are integrated into the church relationally. Yet too often we measure integration merely in terms of their Sunday attendance.

When Revelation Church began in 1983 there were critics who dismissed it as mere "youth church". As the years have passed, the church has grown dramatically and has inevitably aged. What began as a radical expression of church in youth culture gradually became less accessible to young people. As a result, a youth congregation called "Warehouse" was planted back into youth culture. A new generation of young people have been given the space to disciple one another and pioneer new expressions of worship, leadership and evangelism within their own culture groups. However they maintain a high level of relational involvement with the wider church of which they are an expression. In practical terms this is because many of them lodge with church families (a deeper fellowship than a Sunday morning in the same building), our leadership teams flow together and older people sponsor individuals, inviting them round to dinner and parenting them in the faith. As a result, there is a genuine appreciation of the wider body within the youth congregation.

What's more, young people have come to Christ as a result of the culturally relevant evangelism, worship and cell structure that exploded when our student congregation *Warehouse* was started, and are now integrating into a wider body of believers than they would previously have found accessible.

Unity without uniformity

Few people these days doubt the need for new churches to be planted geographically, perhaps on a new housing estate where there is no vibrant Christian witness, or in a village without an evangelical community. However, in today's fragmented communities, there are cultural divides just as real as the geographical ones that necessitate the planting of a new church. This means that it may not be enough simply to go on replicating our existing models of church in numerous locations. We may also need to re-invent ourselves in order to engage with sectors of society on our doorstep that are currently unable to relate to us as we are. This is not just an issue for reaching youth culture, it is an equal challenge for reaching the elderly, the disabled, commuters or a minority race. Generally speaking, expressions of church in the UK are predominantly accessible to white, middle-class and middle-aged cultures. Other social groups struggle to relate and are unlikely to be reached by a weekly act of mass compromise. They need to see the gospel fleshed out in their context and explained in their language addressing the questions posed by their world-view. The church is called to be multicultural, not monocultural, with a unity that is relational and organic, celebrating one another's distinctives together.

Combining colours

Impressionist painters like Monet and van Gogh discovered that by carefully combining thousands of splashes of primary colours they could create a wonderful sense of movement and light. Close-up their pictures can appear chaotic and meaningless, but take a few steps back and suddenly the colours combine to make sense.

In the same way, the church of Christ on the final day will be made up of thousands of cultures, every tribe and tongue, brought together in such a way as to convey the Light of the World. This means that we should feel free to establish churches that look different: indigenous expressions of faith, united in their commitment to Christ but different in the ways they express it. Church is to be one image with many faces and the call to unity has never required uniformity — even at a local level.

After all, if every culture were expected to compromise together all the time, how boring that would be! It would be as though van Gogh had mixed all those bright, primary colours together on his palette, resulting in a dark, muddy monotone, instead of light.

However, the different colours or cultures must still be prepared to relate and work with one another and realistically this does demand a limited measure of compromise. But we should certainly not expect the newest of young converts to be able to suddenly adapt to the alien environment and practices of middle-aged culture or ancient tradition. In fact, it may well take several years for an unchurched teenager to progress from first committing their life to Christ to the point of being willing and able to make the cultural compromises necessary for full integration into wider expressions of church. And if the bridge between conversion and integration into the wider body is too short you actually have a pier and a lot of drowning converts.

Rather than planting youth congregations, some churches are seeking to apply principles of church within their existing models of youth work. This is often because they place a high premium upon the Sunday meeting as a united expression of Christian family in which all ages are represented. Wherever this is working I am delighted; ultimately we must bless wholeheartedly whatever is working in discipling young people — this is no time for missiological narrowness, prejudice or prudishness. However, should churches choose to gather the full spectrum of cultures and ages together each Sunday, there is a clear biblical guideline for them to follow. It is the more mature in Christ who should make the cultural compromises necessary in order to accommodate the rest. The tendency however, is to do the opposite, expecting young people to adapt themselves to fit with church as we have determined it. It's like bringing a new-born baby home, pointing out the fridge and promising to come round twice a week to help in any way at all! Parents know that you have to change your cherished life-style to adapt to that of the newest member, and this is just what God challenges us to do for new and young Christians.

Young people and the arts

When Jesus rode into Jerusalem, crowds lined the streets crying: *Hosanna! — Blessed is he that comes in the name of the Lord!* Agitated by this, the religious leaders told Jesus to shut them up. His retort fascinates me: "*I tell you,*" *he replied,* "*if they keep quiet, the stones will cry out*" (Luke 19:40). We can only guess that the atmosphere as Jesus approached the holy city was so charged with anticipation and longing that he was saying "You can't switch this noise off, you can't make this moment go away, you can't deny the reality of my coming. You have no choice but to face the music! If my disciples do not intercede and worship at such a time as this, then creation itself will pick up the refrain and even inanimate stones will cry out!"

Perhaps we live in days when Christ is once again approaching the city — there is certainly expectancy thick in the air. Could it be that, if the disciples of Christ are intimidated into silence in days like these, inanimate stones; those dead in their sins, will cry out with the longing of the moment? Rock band The Verve sold many thousands of copies of their hit song, *Bittersweet Symphony*. It filled the airwaves with a heart-cry to God: "Well I never pray, but tonight I'm on my knees, I need to hear some sounds that recognise the pain in me."[83]

Many "stones" do appear to be crying out today, declaring a change in the spiritual climate. Secular prophets enshrine the messianic longing of the age in the high street galleries of vinyl, celluloid and image. Perhaps such sights and sounds resonate with creation itself which, Scripture tells us, is groaning for the day when the sons of God will be revealed (Romans 8:19). Youth culture in particular is an effective barometer as to the climate within any society. I have often found that the easiest way of assessing the spiritual temperature of a church is to watch its young people, and you can measure the spirituality of a nation in the same way, provided you come without prejudice.

Young people often have exciting, new ways of thinking which challenge the status quo and threaten to bring change. But all too often the church has resisted such change, squeezing out the creative thinkers who refuse to conform to the required conventions of that particular denomination or congregation. As a result, we have witnessed a sad exodus of those called and gifted young people who — rightly or wrongly — refuse to compromise the identity and ideas that God has given them in order to fit in with rigid church tradition and puritanical opinion. Those that stay behind learn to play the game, to accept and ultimately appreciate, the status quo. Perhaps that is why so many Christian young people are two-dimensional, non-risk-takers, trying to be radical without upsetting anyone!

Having lost so many young people, the church has inevitably surrendered the artistic, prophetic edge it once carried. It seems ironic, though, that the community which represents the creator God should be so bland and alien to most artists while the range of creativity displayed by the rest of society is stunning. But while mainstream art is at times profound and at others depraved, its overall drift is nihilistic. Meaninglessness is held up as the last word in profundity by a world that has pursued its atheism to the final dead end. Art itself comes to nothing as a pile of bricks becomes an eloquent exhibition in the National Gallery. The lives of the artists too are often tragically empty, testifying to the frustration of a gift without a giver, a prophecy without a message, a creation without a creator. Perhaps the greatest tragedy of all is that the church, which was once so rich in creative energy, was not hijacked or robbed of its artistic mantle, but rather we forced out the artists in the name of tradition and convention.

The MTV generation

It was New Year's Day 1998 and I was walking through the beautiful Swedish town of Jonshopping on my way to address a seminar about youth culture. Feeling hungry I walked into a Burger King which looked identical to the one in my home city of Portsmouth. I ordered a meal from the same universal menu, and conversed with the assistant in English before sitting down to eat as a familiar song played on the radio. I arrived at the seminar to find young people wearing the same fashions and with the same range of interests as at home. A photograph of them would not have belied any nationality whatsoever.

There do remain certain important cultural differences from nation to nation, but generally there is an unprecedented degree of common ground among western young people. Wherever I travel I find a shared currency of icons and values. There is, as it were, a world wide web of understanding, an international grid of satellite stations and Internet information and a consensus towards the English language. This unprecedented cohesion within youth culture provides a remarkable opportunity for the spread of the gospel, similar to that offered by the Roman world and language at the time of Christ or the invention of the printing press at the time of the Reformation.

It was one night in Portugal when God first gave me a glimpse of the army that he is gathering; a multitude of young people assembling across the political, denominational and national divides for the honour of his name. I was camping on the most south westerly point of Europe, where the Mediterranean and the Atlantic converge and the rugged Portuguese coastline finally strides into the sea. I couldn't sleep so I crawled out of my lonely little tent to get some fresh air. On this remote peninsula, far from the nearest street lamp, the sky was darker and the stars brighter and more bountiful than the city ever sees. In the distance the moon drew a horizon on the sea like a silver thread. Suddenly I felt very small, touching something very big. The sky soared above me to infinity and the ocean stretched out around me uninterrupted to the vast continents of America and Africa. Turning to face the land mass of Europe, I could picture nation after nation lying before me and I began to pray for each country in turn.

Suddenly there was a sparking, crackling sound overhead and waves of electricity began to buzz through me. Afraid, I looked up, expecting to see a power cable short-circuiting but there was nothing between me and the clear night sky. The power continued to flow as I prayed for several hours for the army of young people that God is gathering. This vision is branded on my imagination to this day.

On October 26th, 1966 Billy Graham addressed the World Evangelical Congress in Berlin with these stirring words: "The evangelistic harvest is always urgent. The destiny of men and of nations is always being decided. Every generation is crucial; every generation is strategic. But we are not responsible for the past generation, and we cannot bear full responsibility for the next one. However, we do have our generation! God will hold us responsible at the Judgment Seat of Christ for how well we fulfilled our responsibilities and took advantage of our opportunities."[84]

Finding ourselves quite by accident at the start of a new millennium we are, I believe, in a uniquely privileged position. The task of reaching our generation with the gospel is certainly daunting, but the opportunities are equally wonderful. With such a wealth of biblical evidence there can be no doubt that God has great dreams for young people today. His heart must break at the pain and despair felt by so many and he longs that his people would prepare and equip churches to gather in the harvest of a generation. These are clearly days of unprecedented opportunity for those willing to approach youth culture as a mission field and not a minefield; those who are prepared to release the potential for change.

CHAPTER 14

I (STILL) BELIEVE IN PREACHING

A lone man dives from the top of a towering dam; a breathtaking free-fall, but for the bungee attached to his ankles. He reaches the bottom, breaks through the skylight of a Russian power-plant and floors a soldier muttering smoothly, "I beg your pardon, I forgot to knock!" Another James Bond film has begun…

We live in a visual world where most people would rather switch on the television than pick up a book. Attention spans seem to be shrinking like the dot of light on an old set. Words are grossly devalued. Political campaigns are won and lost by spin-doctors, manipulating opinions with slick quotes and photo-opportunities. Appearance rules supreme — or so it would appear.

And yet for the church a book remains central to our faith and a half hour sermon generally remains integral to our gatherings. No wonder some people are saying that conventional preaching is out of date in such a multimedia, sound bite culture and that it is our action, our living-out of the Word, that will effectively communicate to today's post-modern audience. But Saint Francis of Assisi hit a more helpful balance when he advised: "Preach Christ at all times, and when necessary use words."

Francis understood that it is fundamentally important to live out the gospel before we give out the words. But there does come a time, even in this visually sophisticated age, when we must speak the words in order to explain our lives and the life of Christ. Peter challenges us: *Always be prepared to give an answer to everyone who asks you to give the reason for the hope that you have* (1 Peter 3:15) The alternative lifestyle of Christ and of his followers will invariably provoke questions from a watching world, and if we are to reap the waiting harvest we must open our mouths and boldly proclaim the message. After all, as Paul points out, unless someone preaches, people will be denied the opportunity to respond (Romans 10:14).

Jesus, living in an ancient middle-eastern society which revolved around oral traditions, combined miraculous *wonders* and gracious *works* with *words* (plenty of them). And Peter, on the day of Pentecost, led three thousand people to the Lord with a fairly long sermon. God had poured out his Spirit with unprecedented power, tongues of fire had rested on unsuspecting heads, languages were being spoken supernaturally and the Christians were staggering around as if drunk. But the greatest power of all was in that first great gospel sermon.

In times of awakening, God has always raised up dynamic, charismatic communicators and one of the inevitable foretastes of the next great awakening, therefore, will be the restoration of the power of preaching and teaching.

The "best show in town"

How tragic it is that so many terminally boring, irrelevant sermons echo around church buildings and school halls Sunday after Sunday. Our Master (whose Spirit is supposed to inspire our communication) was profound, hilarious and shocking. Yet in contrast I have endured talks tedious enough to reduce me to memorising copyright details in the song-book, or even counting the number of dead flies trapped in the fluorescent lighting cases overhead. It seems absurd that we produce and buy best-sellers entitled *101 things to do in a boring sermon* instead of addressing the problem.

The preaching of revival leaders was rarely boring, though admittedly Paul did once send a listener to sleep with disastrous (and miraculous) results (Acts 20:7-12). Revivalists are generally creative, passionate, non-religious, often humourous and acutely relevant in their communication. Among the stories about people being "mysteriously drawn" to hear the gospel in times of revival, it is worth remembering that revival preachers also draw crowds by providing a fascinating diversion from normality. Picture the drama of Wesley standing on his father's tomb to speak. Imagine Whitefield's voice booming out across the moors, full of humour and passion, in an age when ministers only preached in church buildings. Or consider the eccentric William Booth, founder of the Salvation Army, in his peculiar military uniform with the loudest, biggest marching band he could muster. Such men did not shy away from creating a spectacle. We too will have to preach creatively — at times sensationally — if we are to excite a modern audience. Here are a few more great examples:

Better than the horses

George Whitefield once preached with such passion at Hackney Racecourse that a thousand race-goers lost all interest in the horses and listened to him instead!

Brown shoes

What makes a non-Christian teenager go to hear a sermon? Sixteen year old Donald MacPhail went to hear the fiery evangelist at the heart of the Hebridean Awakening, not so much out of spiritual hunger as out of curiosity. He had heard the sensational report that Duncan Campbell dared to wear *brown* shoes (very adventurous in that highly conservative culture where preachers either wore blue or black) and of course he wanted to see for himself! It was also rumoured that Mr. Campbell had once punched the pulpit so hard that it actually broke and those who had experienced the passion of his preaching had no reason to doubt such a thing! MacPhail went back the next night because he had enjoyed the music. Brown shoes, thunderous eloquence and excellent music; in an age before television, these revival meetings offered *the best show in town!*

Fake funerals

I love the story Floyd McClung tells of drawing a crowd in Amsterdam as they marched through its darkened streets in funeral procession. Mourners in black walked slowly through the Red Light District, holding the coffin reverently aloft. Subdued crowds lined the street, pondering on the gloomy spectacle. Some averted their gaze respectfully, but everyone's attention was drawn to that tragic coffin. Suddenly the lid flew open and the corpse jumped to its feet proclaiming the death of sin and the resurrection power of Christ to the bewildered crowd![85]

Blinding a blind man

I recently took a lesson in a local school. As I stood at the front of the class, confronted by stony stares, I came to the brilliant conclusion that they did not want to be in school that day. Finding themselves in school, however, they certainly did not want to study Religious Education. And discovering themselves at school, in an RE lesson, their defiant glares eloquently informed me that they definitely did not want to listen to me. Summoning up all my confidence I attempted a humourous introduction: "Hello, my name's Pete. I'm not a teacher or a terrorist so you don't have to call me sir. I'm married to someone called Sam, but it's OK, she *is* a girl, I've checked..."

There was hardly a snigger. It was so quiet I could almost hear the draught blowing under the door. And then I began describing the story of a blind man who came to Jesus, stumbling and feeling his way along. I described Jesus clearing his throat, gathering a nice mouthful of saliva. "He spat on the ground and mixed up a mud paste. 'What is he doing? Why is he ignoring this poor blind man? Wait a minute, he's not going to... he has... he's rubbing a mucus-and-mud-pie in the poor man's eyes. You could blind someone like that.' Maybe Jesus has gone mad, the pressure has finally got to him. How cruel — to do that to a blind man, I thought Jesus was meant to be nice to people!"

At last the class began to smile as they imagined the scene. After all, it's not very *politically correct* is it? The miracle might not have worked, leaving an embarrassed Jesus to justify the mud-paste incident to the bewildered onlookers, as the unfortunate blind man stumbled away through the crowd.

I described a few more miracles and then asked, "Who would like to see a miracle like that happen, right in front of you?" Like a shot every hand went up and two thousand years vanished in that single instant. The human longing to see God's power has not changed. No wonder people flocked miles on foot into the Galilean countryside to see Jesus on his day off. And they were so excited that one morning *five thousand* of them simultaneously forgot their sandwiches. For them this was undoubtedly the best show in town.

Sizing up the competition

In an age where the world in all it's wonder, humour and depravity can enter our living rooms by remote control, the challenge to the church is a mammoth one. The revivals of Finney, Wesley, Edwards and Campbell all took place in a time before television when many non-Christians still attended church. But how are we, at the dawn of the twenty-first century, to excite and attract a thoroughly secular audience away from the latest soap opera to hear the real-life story of Jesus? We must be even more innovative than those revivalists of the past, with equal passion. We may not be able to compete with the media when it comes to glitz, glamour and cheap thrills, but with God-given creativity, prophetic relevance and signs and wonders following, the crowds will still come.

I had lunch with a television producer who had travelled around England researching creative and exciting churches in youth culture for a series of programmes. He was not a believer and I had one question I was dying to ask him: "What did you make of us?"

His reply surprised and fascinated me: "I have never met a more paranoid bunch of people in all my life! Why are you Christians so suspicious of the media? You seem to find it impossible to believe that you are, in fact, fascinating people: you claim to see miracles, you live radically alternative lifestyles, you seem to know what life's about. The world out there really does want to know all about you."

If we are to attract non-Christians to our events and meetings we must be confident about our message, and we must reverently explore what it means today to "put on the best show in town."

Persuasive preaching

Creative and dynamic communication is essential in attracting a modern audience, but our message also needs to make sense. Creativity is no replacement for content! We must work hard at preaching persuasively, engaging with people's minds and grappling with their world-views.

In my final years at school I was a keen young Christian. I remember one day finding a large and impressive book which finally proved Christianity to be true. As far as I was concerned this one volume was enough to convince anyone and everyone to believe. It showed over hundreds of pages in very small print, with footnotes in even smaller print and without any pictures whatsoever, that the Bible was historically accurate, that the Old Testament predicted the birth, life, death and resurrection of Jesus and probably his sandal-size too.

So I set off to school to show my cynical anti-Christian friend John my tremendous new find. Being an intellectual type who thoroughly enjoyed mangling me with his arguments, he agreed to read it. A few days later a quieter, more sombre John returned the book to me. I could tell it had been read and re-read. "OK I give in," he sighed, "Christianity is obviously true. I guess I'd better become one." You have never seen a more reluctant convert or heard a more depressed rendition of the sinner's prayer.

John only lasted a few weeks trying to be a Christian. The truth is that he had given mental assent, but he had not given his heart; his mind had been convinced but his soul remained unconvicted. He had been persuaded by facts without perceiving the person of Christ.

I learned an important lesson at that time; the whole gospel must engage with the whole person: heart, body and soul as well as mind. However I also made the thrilling discovery that there is a power and credibility in the Bible that can stand up to the closest intellectual scrutiny. I was inspired to study for a degree in Theology, but not at a Bible School where everyone would essentially agree with me for three years, but on a thoroughly secular campus. I wanted to wrestle with the questions that people were really asking, rather than answering questions that no-one was asking, as the church so often can.

A funny little man whose eyebrows met in the middle...

Paul was probably the greatest gospel-persuader of all time. When he arrived in Ephesus he decided to begin his church planting as usual by preaching in the synagogue. We are told that he *spoke boldly there for three or four months, arguing persuasively about the Kingdom of God* (Acts 19:8). When the Jews in the synagogue hardened their hearts,

Paul — undaunted — hired out the local lecture hall where he "had discussions" daily for *two years!* That's a lot of discussing.

According to ancient tradition Paul was short, bald, bow-legged and big-nosed, a funny little man whose eyebrows joined in the middle. Why, then, were people being drawn from all over Asia to see this unimposing figure? Probably because they had heard about the incredible miracles that God was doing through him. Even a slightly bewildered Dr. Luke describes these miracles as "extraordinary". Just imagine the Jews trying to find a Bible verse for healing with hankies! But when they arrived at the lecture hall the crowds found a man *arguing persuasively... holding discussions* (Acts 19:8-10). In spite of all the miracles and the public excitement, Paul was working hard at explaining, relating and debating. Revival does not provide a brain by-pass for thinking sinners.

Sometimes I think we can almost attribute the preaching of the gospel with magical powers, as though a thirty minute rendition of the salvation story should automatically flip some spiritual switch that saves people. Paul, in contrast with such a naive assumption, took two years in a revival atmosphere to discuss and persuade. That is why the primary responsibility for evangelism lies with the local church, and not some short-term team or visiting evangelist. We can take the passage out of context that describes the gospel as "the power of God for salvation", and think that if someone just stands there and recounts the story of the crucifixion, people should somehow respond regardless of background, prayer-cover, screaming babies or the fact that the talk was about as convincing as a politician's smile. Sadly, it's not so easy; the work of an evangelist is just that, work, and it takes time.

Our student congregation Warehouse organised a week of outreach. It was designed to be radical, attractive and exciting. We put on appropriate events in local pubs and conducted a Christian Awareness week in a neighbouring school, with full colour, trendy publicity. Dozens of young people prayed and fasted for three long days. Everything was building towards the Sunday guest meeting which, as usual, was held in one of the local student bars. When the Sunday came there was an excellent turnout and the place was packed with visitors, many of whom had never been to church in their lives before. The meeting was as creative as we could make it with a great band playing, a DJ spinning records, a drama, lights, and a gifted national evangelist speaking. We were trusting God for a massive harvest; we had named it, claimed it and framed it. We thought we had a guaranteed result. After all, we reminded God, the fields are ripe unto harvest… (John 4:35).

The evangelist preached brilliantly to this largely pagan congregation and they listened intently as he clearly communicated the message of the cross. Our counselling team took their positions at the starting blocks, gospel literature crammed in their pockets, tissues at the ready, spiritual grins on their faces. I could imagine the drum-roll in heaven as the evangelist prayed, inviting people who wanted to become Christians to raise their hands. I could visualise the angels clasping their party-poppers, poised to pull the string; I imagined St. Peter preparing the saints for a Mexican-Wave of celebration… Peeping discreetly across the room I could hardly believe what I saw.

From that great congregation not a single hand was raised. Not one. The silence was deafening as we waited for the slightest movement, the tiniest gesture, but no one moved a muscle. I was really disappointed and for a while I thought that God had let us down. It felt a bit like failure.

In the light of the gospel

It was while reflecting on this apparent failure that God spoke to me about Paul in Ephesus. There he was at the height of his heavenly anointing, praying over handkerchiefs to heal people, and yet it still took two years of persistent argument to win the heart of that city. We, on the other hand, were expecting to see major spiritual breakthrough with an unchurched audience in a single evening using a few coloured lights and an initial depiction of the gospel story. Winning that crowd for Jesus is going to take more than a single meeting. The power of the gospel is released to an individual, group, or even a nation, as it is explored and expounded, persistently, persuasively and with integrity.

Those who research into religious experiences say that a majority of the population claim to have had experiences of the supernatural.[86] Rather than instantly rubbishing such experiences as deluded or even demonic (simply because they fall outside the boundaries of our own experience) perhaps we should respect and explore them fearlessly. Preachers would do well to turn the spotlight of Christ onto what non Christians already know and wherever possible to build upon these foundations. This is exactly what Paul did in Athens, using the idol dedicated to an unknown god to introduce Christ. Gospel preaching should never involve telling sinners all that they are not and that everything they think is somehow wrong. Such a presumptuous and unbiblical onslaught gives the gospel a bad name. No wonder Christians get accused of being arrogant, narrow-minded bigots! We must follow the example of Jesus when addressing crowds and use the raw-material of their imagination and collective experience to reveal truth. Within the rubble of a fallen world lies buried the image of our Creator.

There's a beautiful old chorus that goes:

Turn your eyes upon Jesus,
Look full in his wonderful face,
And the things of earth will grow strangely dim
In the light of his glory and grace.

These may be wonderful, poetic words to use in worship, but in some ways they are misleading. It's probably truer to say that in the light of Jesus the things of earth, far from growing "strangely dim", come into sharp focus. G. K. Chesterton pointed out that one does not switch on the light in order to stare at it, but in order to explore what it illuminates. When Christ lights up our lives we receive vital clarity and perspective upon the world around us. Christians should pray more with their eyes open, their televisions on or their music playing, and we certainly need to preach in a way that illuminates and explains the world rather than rejecting or ignoring it. Billy Graham was once described carrying a Bible in one hand and a newspaper in the other. Reflecting on this he wrote: "It did symbolise my constant effort to show the timeliness of God's eternal truths. In preaching the Gospel, I could also comment on everything current — the Communist threat, moral and social issues in the newspapers, Judgment Day."[87] Paul must certainly have grappled with many thorny issues and contemporary questions during the course of his two year residence in Ephesus.

Preaching that is relevant to its audience starts with listening and thinking and the talking, when it comes, will often involve discussion and dialogue as well as the conventional didactic approach of the traditional sermon. Nowhere in Scripture does God indicate that the mechanical recitation of certain historic and spiritual truths has any more power than a reading from the telephone directory. And in revival situations — like Ephesus — the need for "wise and persuasive words" is just as great. At such times there may be a deeper hunger, and a richer anointing but the soul still needs to be won and the mind respected with honest discussion and persuasive argument.

Initiatives like the twelve week Alpha course, which combines excellent preaching with friendly dialogue, have a critical role to play in preparing this nation for revival and will be an invaluable new wineskin as God pours out his new wine. In an increasingly secularised world, we need to release the gospel power through clear thought and great communication as never before. Where are the Whitefields and the Wesleys of our day?

Speaking the right language

We have seen that our preaching should be attractive and persuasive, but it must also be in the right language! We are told that on the day of Pentecost, the people *came together in bewilderment, because each one heard them speaking in his own language* (Acts 2:6). This phenomenon alone left the crowd *utterly amazed... and perplexed... We hear them declaring the wonders of God in our own tongues!*

The power and the passion, the drama and persuasiveness of Peter's great sermon were not enough, his words needed translating. Today's languages are diverse. I'll never forget the bewildered expression on the faces of certain older members of the congregation when a young lad pronounced through the microphone that, in his humble opinion, "God is completely and utterly wicked." Even within a single community people can be speaking very different languages and living in very different worlds. Roger Ellis writes: "If we want to flow with the heart of Pentecost we will be looking to see that the gospel is expressed within all languages. This will heighten our desire to translate, encapsulate and incarnate the gospel to all generations, nationalities and cultures. If we fail to do this ultimately we will end up as an irrelevance. This is not simply a matter of literal languages and cultures but also about some of the sub-cultures that exist within individual nations."[88]

Taking the gospel to every ethnic and cultural sub-group will require far more than just the mechanical translation of one word for another, or the learning of a new set of vocabulary. We must also learn the deeper languages of people's lives, their world-views and their ways of thinking. Jackie Pullinger discovered among the starving heroin addicts of Hong Kong that there was no point in merely translating "Jesus is the Bread of Life" into Cantonese. She had to put rice in their bowls. This was a language they understood.

I worked for a short while with an organisation seeking to communicate God's love to the homeless. Unfortunately, members of staff were expected to dress smartly in shirt, jacket and tie as this was considered a positive witness (although the ties had to be the clip-on variety to reduce the risk of head-butts and strangulation). In return for some food and a cup of tea the homeless visitors were expected to sit through a half-hour sermon, exhorting them to repent and come to Christ. I clearly remember one preacher standing before these rough and ragged souls in his suit and (clip-on) tie illustrating a point by describing driving home after work to his family. Not one of his audience had a car, a job, a home or a close family. His point was good and his intentions undoubtedly kind, but he was not speaking the right language. He was quite possibly hardening hearts in the process.

The language of the masses

Conventional preaching tends to be very middle class in its manner and mentality and has therefore failed to attract the city-dwelling underclasses in any significant number.[89] This irrelevance to the poor is worrying, particularly as we look to the future. By the year 2010 three out of every four people on earth will live in a city,[90] and the majority of those who live there will be underpriviled.[91] Cities have become the global keys to fulfilling the Great Commission. If we are serious about preparing for revival, therefore, we must learn how to communicate effectively with the underprivileged majority who live in cities. Peter Wagner assesses some of the characteristics of effective city-preaching using what he calls The Wilkes Spectrum. This attempts to show clearly (but in highly generalised terms) the difference in personal and Christian preferences between the upper and lower classes. Most people, of course, are somewhere between the extremes listed below.

The Wilkes Spectrum

(Class Preferences for Christian Values)[92]

Personal Preferences:

Intellectual	—	Intuitional
Rational	—	Emotional
Scientific	—	Experiential
Deductive reasoning	—	Inductive reasoning
Literacy essential	—	Literacy optional
You control life	—	Life controls you

Christian Preference:

Intellectual	—	Intuitional
Faith complex	—	Faith simple
Conversion gentle	—	Conversion confrontational
Holiness gradual	—	Holiness sudden
Biblical criticism	—	Biblical literalism
Systematic theology	—	Pragmatic theology
Relative ethics	—	Absolute ethics
Preaching based on study	—	Preaching based on prayer
Weak demonology	—	Strong demonology

The world-wide trend seems to be a movement towards the right side of the spectrum, so unless we reflect this paradigm shift in our preaching we will be increasingly irrelevant. Communication that is relevant to the urban masses will be simple and direct with a strong supernatural dimension. The apostle Paul reminded the Corinthian Christians that *the kingdom of God is not a matter of talk but of power* (1 Corinthians 4:20). Signs and wonders were integral to the preaching of Jesus and of the early church and are similarly exhibited in the ministries of the Argentinean revivalists today. Leaders like Carlos

Anacondia and Omar Cabrera heal the sick, cast out demons and present the message of the gospel to hundreds of thousands of South Americans every single week. We certainly have a great deal to learn from those who are ministering successfully in today's world-class cities. But regrettably, "our theological training institutions in the Western world… talk a great deal about ministering to the poor and oppressed of the world's urban centres in their social ethics classes," but when it comes to the nuts and bolts of "doing church", their world view remains "toward the left side of the Wilkes Spectrum".

Preachers undercover

But preaching the gospel is not just about platforms, microphones and lots of words. It is also about "the Word made flesh"; about communicating with people on their own terms and in their own cultural contexts. With each culture we must set about learning its language so that it can be illuminated by the light of Christ.

Kenny Mitchell is a talented D.J. who uses record decks as his pulpit as he "preaches" regularly in night-clubs. He has a friend who is the complete opposite: Jesus uses him as an academic boffin whose language is mathematical papers and theses that you and I would not even understand! Both of these men are equally radical in reaching out to different people groups. Similarly, bands like DBA and Delirious? are seeking to translate the message of Jesus into the language of the mainstream charts:

> *Well I've got a message to bring,*
> *I can't preach but I can sing*
> *And me and my brothers here,*
> *Gonna play redemption hymns.*[93]

Where are those called to the Internet communities, to the skaters and surfers and Trekkies, to the local squat or the football team, to the fashion industry, the heads of industry, the New Age networks and comedy circuits, not to mention a thousand different offices and schools and pubs and streets?

We desperately need the Spirit's help in declaring the wonders of God in every language today. So often the church has sat contentedly in the upper room, experiencing God's Pentecostal power, praying for the world, trying every technique imaginable for drawing visitors in. But all we really need to do is go, to leave the upper rooms of Christian culture and translate the wonders of God into the languages of today.

Perhaps it is not until we start attending the world's meetings, listening to their teachers and singing their hymns that they will do the same for us. After all, Jesus did not e-mail us from heaven, he did not send a carrier pigeon or even make do with an archangel or two. He came and ate our food, spoke our languages, like us in every way except without sin.

Passionate preaching

We have seen that revivalists will preach creatively, persuasively and powerfully but most of all they must preach with passion.

George Whitefield

George Whitefield was fond of quoting one of the great actors of his day who was asked why his shows attracted such large crowds while most clergymen could only draw meagre congregations. The actor replied that while he took mere fairy-tales and delivered them as though they were in fact true, the clergymen took facts and delivered them as though they were mere fairy-tales! This was certainly not true of Whitefield, who was probably one of the greatest orators England has ever produced. His booming voice was capable of projecting to thousands with such clarity that people a mile away could understand him. He empathised with Baxter who "preached as never sure to preach again, and as a dying man to dying men!"

A young Muslim man told a vicar: "The problem with you Christians is that you seem to lack passion." He knew that any faith forged in the Middle-East should be a thing of fire to be lived out and not just to be analysed and understood. Whitefield's first open-air sermon was a remarkable example of the passion we so often lack.

On Saturday, February 17th 1739, Whitefield stood on a grassy slope in a notorious area of Bristol called Kingswood, and preached his first open air message to two hundred soot-covered miners tramping home. They stopped to hear the young preacher, never having really listened to a minister before, and certainly never having seen one preach in the open-air . On Whitefield's next visit to Kingswood some five thousand people gathered and crowds soon grew to twenty thousand. As he spoke of the cross they were amazed to see tears running down the young preacher's cheeks. And as those tears fell, his words began to penetrate beyond their grime and weariness to a deeper longing to be clean and find rest. Once again, the great and timeless message began to touch dark hearts and Whitefield memorably noticed "white gutters made by their tears down their black cheeks."

Wesley and Edwards

John Wesley travelled some 226,000 miles on horseback, stagecoach and foot, spreading the gospel fires with unquenchable energy and preaching an incredible forty-six thousand times. He would continue in spite of terrible sickness and at times preached with such passion that he vomited blood. On one occasion his horse grew lame and he developed a headache, but on calling out to God both he and his horse were instantaneously healed!

Meanwhile across the Atlantic in New England, Jonathan Edwards preached with such passion that on one occasion "Many of the hearers were seen unconsciously holding themselves up against the pillars, and the sides of the pews, as though they already felt themselves sliding into the pit."

Evan Roberts

Similar passion was a key to the preaching of Evan Roberts in the 1904 Welsh outpouring. "It was not the eloquence of Evan Roberts that broke men down, but his tears. He would break down, crying bitterly for God to bend them, in an agony of prayer, the tears coursing down his cheeks, his whole frame writhing... Evan Roberts, in the intensity of his agony, would fall in the pulpit, while many in the crowd often fainted".[94]

Billy

Tony Campolo tells the remarkable story of another preacher used in revival, far less eloquent but equally consumed. Billy was a kid with cerebral palsy on a Christian Summer Camp in the USA. Others boys on the camp mocked and mimicked Billy's awkward movements and clumsy speech until it made Campolo's blood boil. Each day a different dormitory would choose someone to lead morning devotions, and it soon came to Billy's dormitory to choose. The boys in his group thought it would be funny to make Billy stand and speak to the crowd. The whole camp gathered that morning, and Billy limped slowly to the front as the boys laughed, enjoying the painful spectacle. Billy opened his mouth and, with all the effort and dignity he could muster, began to form words. With agonising slowness he pronounced one simple sentence: "Jesus loves me… and I love Jesus."

Silence had fallen. The Spirit of God hovered over the group. Boys who had moments earlier been mocking were now trembling and sobbing, many on their knees, eyes ashamed. A small revival began in that camp and many were saved, discovering Jesus through the testimony of a disabled kid called Billy who was not ashamed of his Lord.[95]

How desperately this nation needs a new generation of preachers (women as well as men) who will proclaim the Gospel inventively, persuasively and passionately, with minds razor-sharp, tongues attuned to the culture and hearts aflame for God.

IV: PREPARING SOCIETY

Our deepest fear is not that we are inadequate. Our deepest fear is that we are powerful beyond measure. It is our light, not our darkness, that most frightens us. We ask ourselves, "Who am I to be brilliant, gorgeous, talented and fabulous?" Actually, who are you not to be? Your playing small doesn't serve the world. There's nothing enlightened about shrinking so that other people wont feel insecure around you. As we let our light shine, we unconsciously give other people permission to do the same. As we are liberated from our own fear, our presence automatically liberates others.

Extract from President Mandela's inaugural speech, 1994

CHAPTER 15

SETTING THE SCENE FOR A MOVE OF GOD

The work of God is not so independent of human means as it sometimes appears.

Arthur Wallis

God is indisputably sovereign and he will ultimately have his way. But we are equally responsible and have a vital part to play in his plans. On one hand there is no amount of human effort that can generate revival, because it truly is a supernatural thing — a sovereign act of God. But on the other hand it remains tragically evident that the greatest moves of God through history ended not because God had blown some final whistle but rather through human irresponsibility, passivity or sin. This illuminates the fact that revival is not so much something God does to us as something he does with us. We must, therefore, hold these two truths in tension: the sovereignty of God and our human responsibility to act.

This is important to understand because some people try to put God's sovereignty and our responsibility on a sliding scale. They imagine that a high theology of human responsibility somehow detracts from God's sovereignty and so they polarise Christians into those who believe in God's sovereign will, predestination and power on one hand and those who emphasise the human aspects of social engagement, strategy, spiritual warfare, freewill and the power of choice. Duncan Campbell explains the interrelationship between God's will and ours thus: "In the whole field of Christian experience the first step is and remains with God. Thought, feeling and endeavour must all find their inspiration in the sovereign mercy of God... In the field of revival God is sovereign, but I hasten to say that I do not believe in any conception of sovereignty that nullifies man's responsibility. God is the God of revival but we are the human agents through which revival is possible."[96]

In other words, humanity has been given absolute authority within the sovereign purposes of God. He has ordained that there be a remarkable chemistry between his will and ours. How else are we to understand the cosmic implications of Adam's sin, or the awesome eternal consequences of choosing or rejecting Christ?

God's sovereignty

Terry Virgo observes: "Church history can only truly be understood in the context of revivals. There has never been steady development... You can't project a graph into the future and say, 'This is where we are now, so ultimately we'll be over there'. Certainly, we can have our short and long term goals, but church history is wrapped up in the sovereignty of God and in Christ who governs his church."[97]

Although the human responsibility to prepare for revival is a central tenet of this book, I am not suggesting for one minute that we can make revival happen by our own effort. I am convinced that revival is utterly beyond human reach, that Bible teachers cannot teach it in, evangelists cannot preach it in, good meetings don't generate it, zeal and commitment don't achieve it, great churches rarely experience it, and even our intercessors can't seem to pray it in. There is no technique to make revival happen, no secret power switch to be discovered, no formula waiting to be published. This observation is true because the Bible teaches it and because revival history illustrates it, and I know it's true because our church has tried practically *everything* it can think of to make revival happen without success!

Some Christian activists immerse themselves in mission strategy or social action as though these can achieve anything without God's blessing. But ultimately the hope for this world does not lie in evangelistic strategy, Christian television, political lobbying, Alpha dinners, community projects, mission teams, literature campaigns or ecumenical initiatives. Great as all these things are, without the grace of God and a sovereign outpouring of his Spirit the world will remain unreached. We can give our utmost every day of our lives, holding back nothing, and yet still fall short of the calling of God for our lives.

In fact, it seems to be the testimony of those touched by God in revival that it is not until we run out of techniques and come to an end in ourselves, often when Christians are at their most disillusioned and the culture is at its darkest, that God delights to send his power. That way, much as people would like to stand up and claim a little credit, a little glory, they just can't. It's too obvious that they could do nothing and that he has achieved it all.

Before the Argentinean revival many pastors were leading churches of two to three hundred and, try as they might, their congregations seemed to have reached a plateau. When the revival began they found themselves facing congregations of two to three thousand practically overnight. This had nothing to do with a sudden improvement in their leadership skills or a dramatic change in strategy, and had everything to do with a sovereign act of God.

Human responsibility

Without God's supreme acceleration, our frantic efforts will fall far short of revival. But this does not mean that we have to resign ourselves to the hyper-Calvinistic view that "revival will only come when it comes". It seems to me that God is actually waiting for us to play our part in the revival equation and that when we finally do obey — whenever that is — he will graciously send revival.

It is agreed that the ministry of Charles Finney (1821-1875) directly or indirectly brought at least a million people into the Kingdom of God. Equally remarkable is the fact that an estimated eighty-five per cent of Finney's converts stood firm (compared to thirty per cent of Moody's). Finney, with his Arminian-Pelagian outlook, observed a very different law at work in revival from the traditional cyclical theory. He believed that it is always God's will to send revival, but that he awaits passionate prayer and purity on the part of his people. In other words, the church of Jesus Christ runs alongside revival through every generation. The Kingdom of Heaven has been ours for the taking since the resurrection and biblically we have been living in the last days for two thousand years. When we seek revival, therefore, we are not waiting for a chronological moment, preordained in God's diary. Rather we are praying that by faith and obedience we might activate the potential of the present moment.

Finney believed that "we can labour to promote revival with as reasonable a prospect for success as we could find in any other line of work." With disarming simplicity and typical humour he argues that true gospel preaching will reap souls as surely as a farmer who sows seed will reap a harvest of corn.

> *There is a long-held belief that the task of furthering Christianity is not governed by ordinary rules of cause and effect — that there is no connection between tools and results, no tendency in the means to produce the effect. No doctrine endangers the church more than this, and nothing is more absurd. Suppose someone preaches that doctrine to farmers. He kindly explains to them that God is sovereign, and will give them a crop only when it pleases him. Ploughing and planting and labouring as if they expected to raise a crop is very wrong. It takes the work out of the hands of God, interferes with his sovereignty, and works in their own strength. He informs them that there is no dependable connection between their tools, knowledge and resources and the result. Now suppose the farmers believed such a doctrine. We would starve! The same results follow from persuading the church that promoting faithful Christianity is so mysteriously a subject of God's sovereignty that there is no natural connection between the means and the end. What results from such a teaching? Generations and generations, millions of souls, go to hell while the church dreams and waits for God to save the world without using the tools He has given us. This doctrine has been the devil's most successful tool for destroying souls. Yet the connection between means and result is as clear in spiritual things as it is when the farmer sows his grain.*[98]

Naturally supernatural

The Bible teaches that the natural is no less attributable to God than the supernatural. God might heal me inexplicably through prayer or scientifically through medicine; both are supernatural, both are natural. A while ago, my wife Samie and I decided to start trying for a family. We know that children are a precious gift from God, and so we began to pray daily that he would bless us in this way. However, we had to do rather more than just pray! We had a very practical (and not unpleasant) part to play in conceiving. Does this mean that we thank God any less for the child? Of course not! This baby is the most incredible, miraculous, supernatural gift of God we have ever received, but we had a vital part to play, not only in prayer, but also in practice.

It is the awesome testimony of Scripture that God has chosen to need our co-operation and is influenced by our choices just as we are by his. God abandoned his destructive plan for Nineveh when they repented (much to the dismay of Jonah) and Moses even persuaded God to change his mind (Exodus 32:14). Behind such texts the very narrative of Scripture is one of relationship and interaction between God and humanity. The Bible does not reveal God as "a metaphysical iceberg",[99] unchanging, unyielding and unbending in his will. Instead it shows that people have a vital part to play in triggering and even shaping God's sovereign plans. Noah was given practical instruction how to build the ark. Did this detract from God's sovereignty in sending floods? Of course not! But without Noah's obedient preparation God's plans would have been thwarted, such is the awesome partnership that he has with his people. The ultimate expression of God's sovereignty in sending Jesus was predicted by the prophets, prayed for by Simeon and prepared for by his cousin John. Even Mary had to say, "I will".

Christ reveals the great mystery of a Creator who submits his will to the created. From the helplessness of the nativity to the selflessness of the cross, we can only wonder at a God whose ultimate power flows from submission, whose sovereignty is expressed in surrender and whose purposes are achieved through failure. The message of the cross is that God's sovereign rule is not fragile like that of a business manager, reigning monarch or classroom bully who simply have the power to make people obey them. God's power is far deeper and more unshakeable than that, rooted in love and surrender. At first glance this can seem an immeasurably greater risk but since even attack and hatred result in God's glory, one way or another all creation does indeed glorify its creator — even those parts that are attempting to rebel!

It is a truth, buried in the heart of God's sovereignty that he has chosen to rule through co-operation and even surrender to the will of man. He does not rule for the love of power but rather, with the power of love by which he submits himself to his bride.

In the light of all this, it is a naive form of Christian fatalism that does nothing, waiting helplessly for God to send revival. I would suggest that such passivity flows from a misunderstanding of God's sovereignty which leaves us powerless pawns in his will. In sharp contrast with this unbiblical understanding of the relationship between God's activity and ours, the parable of the talents clearly teaches that if we sit around and do nothing with the gifts and graces that God has already given us we will be severely judged. Such servants are described as "wicked" and "lazy" (Matthew 25:26).

Another problem with the cyclical view of revival as an occasional, preordained season is that it can breed a sense of hopelessness and helplessness in churches that find themselves "between revivals", in which case there is little to do but wait patiently for the next season of power, hoping that one is scheduled for your lifetime and your locality. Even prayer may seem something of an empty duty if God's preordained moment has not yet appeared upon the horizon.

It seems vital to me that Christians recognise the part they have to play in preparing society for revival. God's Spirit needs a body, his river needs banks. Jesus told one of his harshest parables to warn us against failing to get ready for him. He describes the return of a brutal master to find that the servant he left in charge has mismanaged his estate: *The master of that servant will come on a day when he does not expect him and at an hour he is not aware of. He will cut him to pieces and assign him a place with the unbelievers. That servant who knows his master's will and does not get ready... will be beaten with many blows... From everyone who has been given much, much will be demanded, and from the one who has been entrusted with much, much more will be asked* (Luke 12:46-48).

We have here a sober warning to live our lives alert and ready for Jesus. We are called to actively prepare, to use our common sense like the five wise bridesmaids who remembered to bring extra oil for their lamps as they waited for the bridegroom (Matthew 25:1-13). The other bridesmaids did not think ahead and so they were not ready when the groom appeared. The lamps Jesus describes in this story needed replenishing with oil every fifteen minutes. No wonder Jesus describes those who forgot to bring fuel as "foolish"; they were not even thinking fifteen minutes ahead! As we prepare for revival and ultimately for Christ's return let us not be foolish and fail to plan, strategise and think ahead. But rather let us seek to be wise, getting our communities and ourselves ready for the coming King.

The sociology of revival

My garden is tangled with weeds. I can pull them out, bury them and drown them in poisonous chemicals and they just love it. Occasionally a foolish whim overtakes me as I drive past one of the garden centres currently self-seeding all over the known world, and I rashly purchase an attractive plant (a really healthy one) taking it home proudly to plant. Clearing away the weeds I follow the advice on the pot meticulously; watering it, feeding it (and occasionally, I confess, even praying for it). But the inevitable always happens. Within days that carefully cultivated bloom looks as though it has been microwaved, while the resurrected weeds just laugh at me. I am told that this is because the soil's acidity level is ideally suited to weeds but not, it seems, to plants you pay for (and even pray for). I am also told that it is because I am bad at gardening.

Revivals, like plants, thrive in the right soil. They need certain sociological, historical and cultural contexts to flourish. Peter Wagner, the church growth expert and author who has observed revival scenarios around the world, comments: "All church growth is a complex interweaving of contextual factors, institutional factors and spiritual factors." Christians tend to be good at recognising and expounding the spiritual factors, but not so good at recognising the contextual and institutional ones. Our revival accounts often gloss over the human elements, wary (I suppose) of detracting from God's glory. But until we are honest about the sociological factors that have set the scene for every awakening, people will continue to delegate responsibility, assuming that the next one will just materialise out of nowhere.

The Bible teaches that God raises up kings, queens and even presidents, and the Old Testament conveys as many rules relating to social interaction and community life as to worship and prayer. It shows us a God who is concerned about, and caught up in, culture and social interaction. We have a responsibility not just to pray, but also to generate an atmosphere of receptivity to the gospel in our culture, here and now.

Hebrides

I want to take as an example the Hebridean awakening. Having read so much about the spontaneous outpouring that sparked the revival, I journeyed there to discover more. I was surprised, but encouraged, to learn that this work of God was not nearly so independent of human means as many of the accounts imply. Prior to the awakening, there had been a spiritual dryness facilitated by various human criteria, which meant that when the sparks of revival fell they soon became a spreading wildfire.

The sense of community and family on the Hebridean islands is significantly stronger than on the mainland. Native islanders will have one of about four surnames, so revival is free to spread through their close-knit families and communities in a way that is less likely in our broken and dislocated localities. This is not to say that revival is any less possible for an almighty God in today's culture but it does challenge us to build community and invest in family as we prepare for revival.

The Hebridean culture was very conservative, owing partly to its geographical isolation, and it was God-aware and God-fearing to an unusual degree. For instance, children were still taught passages of Scripture and the *Shorter Catechism* at school. This meant that when the rain of revival fell, these dry and dormant seeds of truth quickly grew into a great harvest.

Another sociological consideration must be that, in relatively isolated communities before television, there was not much to do other than work. So the fiery young preacher who wore brown shoes proved an attraction that he might not have been in the cities on the mainland.

A final consideration must be that the islanders had lost a disproportionately large number of men in the war, just four years previously, and that there was a sense of pain and an awareness of eternity in the lives of many that made them unusually receptive to the gospel.

Argentina

Sociological factors were equally evident in contributing to the massive Argentinean awakening of recent years. Traditionally Argentina had proved to be one of the hardest mission fields for Protestant mission, that is until the Falklands war of 1982. "The British victory caused a radical change in Argentinean social psychology. National pride, for which the Argentines were internationally notorious, was severely damaged. The church had failed them, the military had failed them, Peronism had failed them — they were ready to try something new".[100]

John the Baptist

Sociopolitical forces undoubtedly set the scene for John the Baptist's awakening cry. A popular Bible commentary describes "the intense religious excitement and social ferment of the early days of John the Baptist's ministry. Herod had been rapacious and extravagant; Roman military occupation was harsh. Some agitation centred around the change of procurators from Curatus to Pilate in AD 26. Most of the people hoped for a religious solution to their political fortunes, and when they heard of a new prophet, they flocked out into the desert to hear him."[101]

Like every revivalist before and since, John the Baptist clearly had more than just the right message; he had it at the right time.

Scotland

In 1739 the Scottish parish of Cambuslang experienced an eclipse of the sun followed by severe storms, a wet harvest and a terrible winter in which two thousand people died. Responding to this tragedy the Glasgow Presbytery called a day of "solemn humiliation, fasting and prayer", and William McCullock, minister of Cambuslang fostered the mood of pain and piety with weekly lectures and daily prayer meetings. As a result within a year one third of his parish had been converted. What's more, McCullock's diligent ministry in the wake of such natural disasters set the scene for a gathering of thirty to fifty thousand people on 15th August 1741 to hear George Whitefield at the (now famous) Cambuslang communion. This momentous gathering had not materialised from thin air, but rather had been forged in the furnace of social upheaval.

Azusa Street

The Azusa Street outpouring which gave birth to the world-wide Pentecostal movement also began in the wake of a natural disaster which had sensitised the spirit and shattered the security of many. On Wednesday 18th April 1906 a terrible earthquake shook San Francisco and the surrounding region killing more than five hundred people. The next day further tremors rocked the city, spurring many to consider eternity and it was in this atmosphere, the day after the quake, that the first inauspicious meetings began at Azusa Street, which went on to shake the world. Here, once again, we see the important chemistry between sociological and spiritual factors in the genesis of revival.

Such factors cannot generate an awakening, but they undoubtedly set the scene for a sovereign move of God. In the next two chapters we are going to explore ways in which we can shape the sociological landscapes of today in preparation for the return of Christ.

CHAPTER 16

GHETTO BLASTERS

It is time to prepare ourselves for an unprecedented revival, it is time to prepare ourselves for the changing of the guard in every area of life, all over the world. Our preparation must help us answer the question: I'm saved; what now?[102]

The irreverent English comedian Paul Whitehouse, in his hit series *The Fast Show* depicts "the inappropriate Christians." A distressed woman enters a police station to report her dog missing and the reception officer takes her details.

"And the dog's name, madam?"

"Jess."

"Jess? That sounds rather like Jesus, madam."

The unfortunate dog owner discovers that the police station is staffed entirely by "born-again" Christians. She watches bewildered as they embrace, sing choruses with a folk guitar and even "get caught up in the love of the Lord." Eventually she manages to file her complaint and issue a description of the dog thief.

"Well madam, the good news is that we detained a man answering to that description earlier today."

"Oh wonderful!"

"And the even better news is that we forgave him and let him go!"[103]

Sketches like that can be almost too close to the truth for comfort but it certainly does us no harm to laugh at ourselves from time to time. However, I have a sneaking suspicion that this scenario unwittingly parodies some people's vision of an awakened society. They anticipate a world in which every school, office and, yes, every police station, is populated by guitar strumming Christians being nicer than Mother Teresa to each other. They imagine that, come revival, every pop lyric will rhyme with Jesus (not easy), every blazer will boast a fish badge and every tannoy system will intone the latest praise tune. Such a vision is, of course, a superficial caricature of the redemption that Jesus actually died to bring.

Revival must impact the communities and social structures of the world in which we live. But the "Inappropriate Christians" force us to question what such a revived world should actually look like. What does the "Kingdom come" mean in practice if you are an insurance broker, shop assistant or policeman? And what are we actually envisaging when we ask God to save our nation?

The fruit of an outpouring of God's Spirit upon society should have nothing to do with fish stickers on every used car or super-spiritual unreality. Rather it should enhance communication, encouraging greater professionalism, fair wages, servant management and conscientious employees. There should be increased care for the poor, respect for the elderly and a reduction in hospital waiting lists. Bewildered newspapers would announce that crime and divorce rates are plummeting, that the streets are becoming safer and that there is a renaissance in the arts. Such wonders surely mark the Kingdom of Heaven, first fruits of a new earth.[104]

Full time ministry

It is high time that we faced the fact that there is no biblical hierarchy of vocations in the Kingdom of God. The Reformation established the truth that every single believer from bus-driver to bishop is a priest, and that we are all in full-time Christian ministry. This means that it is just as godly to spend your life as a housewife or a mechanic as to lead a church or serve on the mission-field.

Despite this fact, we persist in referring to those who draw a salary for Christian work as "full-time" and even distinguish some of them as priests! This points to the fact that deep down we still view some jobs as more spiritual, more "ministry", than others. It also implies that the vast majority of Christians who work on the front line of secular employment are not called to minister in that context. It suggests that their work place, filled as it is with lost souls and complex ethical dilemmas, is of less interest to God than church.

Jesus spent a surprisingly small amount of his time in religious contexts, and when he did visit the temple or synagogues he often got into trouble. The majority of his ministry was spent identifying with accountants, housewives, fishermen and carpenters, forcefully advancing his Father's Kingdom through subversive teaching, miracles of liberation and sacrifice. Jesus' understanding of what it means to be in "full-time ministry" was clearly far broader than ours!

The original biblical word for ministry simply describes any act of giving or serving, regardless of context. That is why, in the first recorded instance of ordination to the Christian ministry, the newly appointed ministers' job description was simply to wait on tables (Acts 6:4). The very same Greek word that is used here to describe the ministry of serving food is used two verses later to describe the apostles' ministry of serving the word. This means that waitressing can be a spiritual act of ministry just as much as preaching and teaching the Bible. Donald Kraybill points out: "We do not have two gospels — one spiritual and the other social, one concerned with salvation and another concerned with hunger. We have a single, integrated gospel, the gospel of the Kingdom".[105]

Christians are called to minister God's reconciliation in every situation they enter, and not just in church contexts (2 Corinthians 5:18). The call to minister within the church is particularly important, however, but it is the task of every Christian and not just the remit of those paid to maintain such a focus full-time. There is also a gospel compulsion to exercise ministry among the poor and marginalised because they represent Christ in our midst. All this places a tremendous responsibility upon every believer to approach the whole of life, regardless of context, as full-time ministry.

It is easy to believe all this as sound theology without really grasping its implications for our own lives and churches. Tom Marshall, the late Bible teacher and business consultant, taught that evangelists may well be those who have gifts in marketing and selling, prophets probably carry valuable creative vision and business insight, pastors have gifts for the caring professions and so on. Where then will we deploy such gifted ministries? The answer is one of specific calling and common sense. Some people are clearly called to apply such gifts primarily within the church but most should do so in broader social contexts.

A young, enthusiastic Christian was offered a job working for a lively church which would have carried quite a lot of social kudos. It was an attractive offer, but he felt called rather to minister evangelistically in a sales job and on the local rugby team. Two years later God is using and blessing him in these contexts.

A key member of our church is currently training to cycle competitively at a very high level. He might even make it to the Olympics. It can sound more spiritual to lead a Bible-study than to ride a bike, but the fact is that God has given him an exceptional ability and we have a responsibility to release him from certain church commitments to pursue his dream. It is not just an obligation towards him as an individual, however, but also towards society and the world of sport.

A gifted computer programmer with the ability to win lucrative contracts feels called to devote himself full-time to pastoring the church. For years he has used his computer skills to finance his dream of devoting more time to believers. We have talked with him and believe that God is indeed calling him out of "the market-place" and onto the pay roll of the church. The issue is always one of calling and common sense, and has nothing to do with one area being more spiritual than any other.

But if every Christian is called to full-time ministry, what does this mean in practice beyond just being a good Christian witness at work? What are we actually supposed to be ministering in our various communities?

Ministers of liberation

The call of the gospel of Christ is to advance the Kingdom in society. However this can sound rather imperial, as though we are somehow trying to conquer resistant communities and hoist the flag of Christendom regardless. No wonder society is nervous of revival. Andrew Marr, when he was editor of *The Independent* newspaper, told

Third Way magazine that in his opinion the very last thing Europe needs right now is another Evangelical awakening. If he expects us to start strumming guitars in police stations whilst pressuring people into our camp, I'm not surprised that he feels that way.

Walter Wink, in his book *Engaging the Powers*,[106] helpfully points out that our call is not to dominate the earth but to liberate it. There is an important difference here. The earth is already the Lord's, but a dictator currently oppresses everything in it. We wage war with the oppressor (Ephesians 6:12) but make peace for the oppressed. There is no license to simply replace one domination with another, no matter how much more benevolent our master is. There are only free slaves in this Kingdom because our Creator credits us with such an awesome power of choice.

Jesus came to proclaim freedom to the captives and Paul wrote that "it is for freedom that Christ has set us free" (Galatians 5:1). In other words we are freed "for" and not just "from" something. By liberating communities from the tyranny of Satan, we enable individuals to make free choices as to whom they will serve. We are not called so much to convert people, therefore, as to empower them to make right decisions. "Empowerment is to be taught how to think, not what to think. It is to be enabled to shape the destiny of your own life for the benefit of those around you… Empowerment is about allowing people to make up their own minds, even if they disagree with you, and respecting them for it."[107]

Most of the population is currently too oppressed to choose Christ. In Irvine Welch's movie *Trainspotting*, the heroin-addled anti-hero Renton chants the mantra: "Choose life… but why would I want to do a thing like that?" If we are to see awakening once again we will have to minister sufficient liberty to enable people to choose freedom and life. We will have to unlock the possibilities so that people can choose as free agents.

Culture shaping

John the Baptist preached personal piety. But he also spoke out against social injustice. In fact he so threatened the cultural status quo that Herod had him imprisoned. John shows us that it is not sufficient simply to prepare the way of the Lord in our hearts and our churches.

We must also clear the highway of contemporary culture so that society can receive the coming King. In other words we must help society to want Jesus; which is not nearly as impossible as it might sound.

One of the great spiritual shifts in the last twenty years has been the rise of the New Age movement. Fusing eastern monism with western paganism it touches most areas of modern life. You might find a teenage girl consulting her horoscope in the playground while her mother attends a yoga class, her brother sticks a yin yang symbol on his school bag and her dad unwittingly absorbs monistic philosophy on a Management Training Course at work. This new pluralistic atmosphere could well prove a far more fertile mission field for the church than the rocky terrain of rationalism that preceded it. Many of our young people have come to Christ out of such backgrounds already. But the process by which such scientifically tenuous, and occasionally ludicrous New Age beliefs have managed to enter the popular mainstream so quickly, is highly relevant to those interested in stimulating another swing in public spirituality, towards Christ.

The counter-culture grows up and buys a Volvo

In the 1960s and 70s a generation of mainly middle-class young people grew their hair, experimented with cannabis, advocated free love and opted out. Their imagination had been captured by the hippie ideal of men like Timothy Leary, and they pushed back the boundaries of experimentalism and permissiveness, determining to live their lives differently, counter-culturally and even spiritually. On graduation from university many cut their hair and landed top jobs, but beneath the new respectability their world-view remained the same. Twenty years on, those who once "tuned in and dropped out" are now the middle aged pillars of society. They have become the politicians, the journalists, the image-makers and the entrepreneurs who generally dictate the way that society thinks. In an age where more is spent world-wide on advertising than on education, it is not over-cynical to say that these people now extensively determine mainstream thought.

In just twenty years an alternative world-view has come right to the heart of society. This should inspire us with wonderful hope. The lessons to be learned are clear:

1. We must strategically resource student ministry, because whoever captures the heart of today's campuses has already shaped tomorrow's world.[108]
2. Christians must aggressively pursue long-term positions of cultural influence. On D-Day the Allied Forces invading France discovered that the Resistance Army had been bravely preparing the land for their coming for years. We need those who will go undercover for Christ, transforming society from within as catalysts of change. This ministry will prepare the way for revival to engage with culture when it comes, ministering liberation wherever it goes.

There are certain areas of society that are disproportionately influential; particularly those within the mass media, television production, journalism and advertising. Add to this the arts and politics and you have a familiar role call of zones from which the church has traditionally retreated in the name of purity. Bands like Delirious? are pioneering into these areas by releasing records into the mainstream charts, seeking to be credible Christians in the entertainment industry. Those that accuse them of selling out for the sake of fame are missing the point entirely. Until Christians brave the high ground of public influence, other ideologies will continue to captivate the masses, and our attempts at evangelism will continue to be met with a great deal of resistance and suspicion. Successful Christian musicians, politicians and journalists are called to be salt and light (Matthew 5:13-16) in places of influence and not to abuse their position by constantly preaching. After all, no-one wants to sit down and eat a plate of salt, but the tiniest amount of skilful seasoning can make a meal irresistible!

During the Second World War a German prisoner of war was sent to work on the grounds of a large English country house near Oxford. Surprisingly, he laboured away diligently, without complaining or attempting to escape for the duration of the war, and after the Allied victory he was sent home to Germany. One morning, the following spring, the butler glanced out of the window to see that the vast flower bed, into which the prisoner had poured so much careful effort, had finally blossomed into an enormous and defiant swastika. The job of shaping the mind-set of this nation will take a great deal of effort and time. But if the church will commit and envision its best people to sow into the hardened soil of society, I believe that God will once again promote many as influencers in his name; heroes like Daniel, Nehemiah and Esther.

Restocking the shelves

When my wife was pregnant, she experienced a remarkable array of food cravings that seemed to change from one moment to the next. Sometimes she couldn't work out what it is she so desperately wanted to eat until we drove past the appropriate take-away or wandered like pilgrims down the aisles of our local supermarket. Our post-Christian neo-pagan culture is a bit like that. Most people are aware of an acute spiritual hunger, but they cannot identify what it is they crave, and so they fill themselves with things that fail to satisfy. Tragically they are unaware that Christianity is still even on the menu of possibilities. It is as though the Bread of Life has been withdrawn from supermarket shelves. People have been persuaded by the subliminal prejudices of the culture shapers that science somehow disproves Christian faith, that "normal" people don't believe "that stuff any more", or that Jesus is irrelevant to modern existence.

There is a crying need for Christians to restock society with an awareness of the gospel. Realistically, this can be achieved with medium-term investment into strategic areas of local and national life. By itself culture-shaping cannot generate revival, which remains a supernatural transaction, but it can make the evangelism of ordinary Christians like you and me much easier, by sensitising society to look for its Creator in the right places.

CHAPTER 17
SOCIAL JUSTICE

The great business of the church is to reform the world — to put away every kind of sin. The Christian church was designed to make aggressive movements in every direction, to lift her voice and put forth her energies against iniquity in high and low places, to reform individuals, communities and governments, until every form of iniquity is driven from the earth.

Charles G. Finney, *23rd Lecture on Revival*

Emergency on planet earth

Our world is in a state of emergency:

- In China there are more than 250 million unemployed, which is more than the entire population of the United States.[109]
- In Brazil between 1995-1996 an area of rain forest the size of Ireland was destroyed.[110]
- In Thailand an estimated 800,000 girls aged between twelve and sixteen are involved in prostitution.[111]
- In the UK every single household currently spends an involuntary £28.45 per week on weapons.[112]
- In Africa an estimated 7.5 million children will die from, or be orphaned by, HIV by the year 2000.[113]
- The suicide rate among British males aged between fifteen and twenty-four jumped a massive seventy-one per cent between 1982 and 1992.[114]
- Today, as you read this, almost forty thousand children will die needlessly as a result of malnutrition or preventable disease,

which is equivalent to eighty Boeing 747s crashing daily, without survivors.

Such statistics can leave us feeling numb, guilty and helpless; the concepts can be too much to grasp. But as we turn the pages of the Bible, it becomes clear that our God is intimately involved in these situations and that he calls his people to engage with the world's pain too. He burns with anger against oppressors and with tender compassion for those they oppress. In today's global village it is, therefore, meaningless to talk of revival unless it relates to the pain and poverty of our neighbours. Our hope for revival is wonderful but as Augustine wrote, "Hope has two beautiful daughters. Their names are anger and courage; anger at the way things are, and courage to see that they do not remain the way they are."

Three of the most obvious results of revival are church growth, increased piety and a release of worship to God. But justice is integral to all three of these fruits, right at the heart of the Kingdom come.

Revival results in growth

Revival will result in dramatic church growth, but we must ask an unusual question about such increase: what is the purpose that makes expansion worthwhile? A student visited Columbia to work with a large church in a deprived area. They conduct excellent meetings with wonderful times of worship and are growing fast. Sadly and surprisingly, however, she discovered that they are doing nothing about the poverty that exists on the doorstep of their auditorium. The church's middle-class membership drives in from the suburbs and the pastor lives in a security-guarded penthouse.

In stark contrast, Rosie came across a tiny gathering of Christians meeting nearby in the broken heart of the slums. Their meeting place is a dilapidated building where the local Mafia boss grants them protection, because they are educating her son. The singing at these church meetings is tuneless, but they do so at the top of their voices through loud speakers deliberately angled out onto the street. This small group is ministering God's love powerfully and practically in this dispossessed community.

Let me say that both churches experience the presence of God, and that he loves the middle-classes as much as the marginalised, but there can be little doubt which community reflects his earthly ministry more closely. The American author Bill Bryson notes his nation's craving for more of everything, from monster "snacks" to Sunday papers "thick enough to stop a bullet". Commenting on this he writes: "More isn't better. It's just more."[115] Every church should have this engraved somewhere prominent. While labouring in the harvest fields we should never forget that in God's eyes numbers are not necessarily success.

Growth in and of itself is not necessarily a good thing; that depends on what is being increased. If a church, however small, is making a radical difference in its community then growth will be wonderful because it will result in an increase of that valuable ministry. But if a church is doing little for its non-members, and membership itself is primarily a matter of attendance, what is the practical benefit of growth?

Revival results in righteousness

As well as resulting in church growth, revival will be branded by the consecration of God's people. It is interesting to note, therefore, that in Scripture the word for righteousness can generally also be translated "justice". The concept of personal piety is inseparably interwoven with the issues of corporate righteousness and social action. In other words, holiness is not just a matter of avoiding sin and praying a lot. It is also fundamentally to do with the way we respond to the poor and the marginalised.

Revival results in worship

But revival will not only generate church growth and righteousness. It will also result, most wonderfully of all, in great glory to God. But does this just mean lots more people singing songs to God on Sunday? Old and New Testament prophets make clear that the worship God requires of us is first and foremost to do with justice. Micah asked the question: *With what shall I come before the Lord and bow down before the exalted God?* (Micah 6:6). His startling response is that God does not particularly enjoy the conventional sacrifices, but rather requires worshippers *to act justly and to love mercy and to walk humbly with your God* (Micah 6:8).

Micah is echoing a theme prophesied by Isaiah: *Is not this the kind of fasting I have chosen: to loose the chains of injustice and untie the cords of the yoke, to set the oppressed free and break every yoke? Is it not to share your food with the hungry and to provide the poor wanderer with shelter…?* (Isaiah 58:6-7). The Lord is not interested in empty fasting, prayer or sacrifice. Presumably he is equally unimpressed by worship songs sung repeatedly without reflection or Bible studies conducted without obedience. The worship that God appreciates is the glory of lives committed to justice and compassion; *Then your light will break forth like the dawn, and your healing will quickly appear; then your righteousness will go before you, and the glory of the Lord will be your rear guard* (Isaiah 58:8).

The justice of Jesus

In the parable of the sheep and the goats, Jesus made clear that acts of mercy towards the oppressed are in fact acts of kindness done to him. This means that the poor in our communities actually represent Jesus and our response to them says a great deal about our response to the Lord himself.[116] Greg Valerio summarises the message of this parable: "We can be sure that in the end Jesus will not ask us what we did with our houses, our careers, our church buildings or how much we tithed. Jesus will be more concerned about our response to the marginalised and the poor, as Matthew so clearly hi-lights."[117]

Even Jesus' birth made a radical statement about God's priorities. He was born in the dirt and chill of a stable and laid in an unhygienic food trough. His arrival, though heralded by angels was witnessed by shepherds and some foreign astrologers who turned up one day with the cheerful little gift of burial spices (not exactly a conventional baby shower). It was hardly an auspicious start. But right from his moment of conception in an unmarried mother, to the moment of crucifixion between criminals, God bound himself to the poor and the marginalised. From the cradle to the grave, God's humble, broken heart could find no other expression. No wonder the gospel is good news to the poor.

Wealthy people on the other hand, have a vested interest in ignoring this scriptural bias towards the poor. Mrs Alexander's famous hymn *All things bright and beautiful* depicts "the rich man in his castle, the poor man at his gate; God made them high and lowly and ordered their estate". The mechanisms by which the privileged avoid the implications of God's bias to the poor often involve spiritualising Jesus' life and teachings. For instance, western Christians tend to understand the Bible's one hundred and seventy-seven references to poverty as spiritual rather than material hardship. Similarly, when Jesus talks about bringing "sight to the blind", sighted people tend to interpret it in terms of "spiritual blindness", in spite of the fact that only eleven of the New Testament's fifty references to blindness were meant this way. A preacher once expounded the story of Zacchaeus by saying that Jesus wants to remove us from the spiritual trees we hide ourselves in. He informed his listeners that if they were ever unfortunate enough to get *treed*, they could still be *freed* by Jesus. Donald Kraybill writes: "A more realistic reading of the text sees a rich exploiter who meets Jesus, repents and immediately corrects the economic injustice he caused."[118]

Throughout Jesus' ministry he consistently confronted injustice and deliberately engaged with the neediest people. In fact he tells us that the Spirit of the Lord is upon him for the purpose of lifting the poor, liberating the oppressed and healing the blind (Luke 4:18-19).

In the beatitudes Jesus laid out the alternative manifesto of the Kingdom: to be a community populated by the poor, hungry, grieving and insulted. In Luke's account he even adds a stern warning to the privileged and popular: *But woe to you who are rich, for you have already received your comfort. Woe to you who are well fed now, for you will go hungry. Woe to you who laugh now, for you will mourn and weep* (Luke 6:24-25). Elsewhere he talks about the difficulty for a rich man to enter the Kingdom.

Perhaps we should be less surprised, therefore, that awakening is more common in the poorer parts of our world today since it has always been the poor who have hosted Christ most comfortably. While we expound yesterday's revival in books, they experience it today in their lives. Jackie Pullinger, in her remarkable ministry to the poorest communities of Hong Kong, repeatedly enthuses that if you want to see revival, you should "plant your church in the gutter".

One of the most dramatic examples of these priorities is Jesus' forceful eviction of the corrupt money-makers that were exploiting foreign pilgrims in the temple courts — actions which would today be worthy of arrest. Then straight after confronting this religious hypocrisy, Jesus finds himself surrounded by handicapped adults and chattering children, whose innocent, unwitting worship contrasts sharply with that of the money-lenders. This is a vivid picture of the difference between Jesus' Kingdom values and the Temple's religious rituals. While false religion discriminates against the poor, the true religion of Jesus welcomes and favours them (see James 1:27). No wonder Kraybill in his excellent book describes this as "the upside-down Kingdom".

The church of the poor

These inverted values continued at the very heart of early church life. The church in Jerusalem was marked out by its sacrificial generosity towards the poor: *Selling their possessions and goods, they gave to anyone as he had need* (Acts 2:45). As a result, Luke can make the remarkable observation that *there were no needy persons among them* (Acts 4:34). This becomes even more of an achievement when you reflect that such a community would have been like a magnet for those in need, as word spread that this crazy Jesus sect would give whatever they had!

When the twelve apostles first appointed other leaders it was to provide a better service for widows and orphans (Acts 6:3), which says a great deal about the priorities modelled by the earliest believers. It is also a profound challenge to the agenda of most churches today.

In AD 360, the backslidden emperor Julian grudgingly acknowledged the extraordinary generosity of Christians towards the poor. He wrote with evident frustration: "It is their benevolence to strangers, their care for the graves of the dead and the pretended holiness of their lives that have done most to increase their atheism… the impious Galileans support not only their own poor but ours as well!"[119] He goes on to chastise his pagan priests for failing to inspire even a hint of such selflessness in their adherents.

The gospel has always been good news to the poor. During the Evangelical Awakening, George Whitefield deliberately carried the gospel to the very poorest people he could find. In fact his first sermon was in the most deprived area of Bristol shunned even by the labouring classes, where miners lived in dirty hovels like "sheer heathens… utter savages". He then singled out the notorious yards of the glass factories and London's Kennington Common, the site of public hangings, not to mention "the brewer's draysmen and fish porters of this naughty world". The nobility who also flocked to hear Whitefield were forced to fraternise with the poor, though in the event many hid in their coaches! Whitefield established an orphanage and school for one hundred and fifty children in Bethesda and single-handedly raised the money to finance it throughout his ministry.

Church and society

In 1943 Lutheran pastor Dietrich Bonhoeffer was arrested by Hitler for smuggling fourteen Jews to Switzerland. In 1939 he had bravely rejected an invitation to flee Germany at the outbreak of war, convinced that his Christian duty was to stay and resist the apparent injustices of Nazism. After imprisonment he was eventually hanged on 9th April 1945 at the age of 39. While in prison he wrote about a "religionless Christianity" which dares to live not by middle class values but rather by the Sermon on the Mount. Indeed, he prophesied that: "The renewal of the church will come from a new type of monasticism which only has in common with the old an uncompromising allegiance to the Sermon on the Mount. It is high time men and women banded together to do this".[120] One of the great failures of the modern western church has been its inability to engage with society's injustice and poverty. This impotence can be traced back to clear historical, theological origins, which are important for contemporary Christians to be aware of and indeed beware of. These centre on the chemistry between church and society.

In the nineteenth century, liberal theologians such as Albert Schweitzer argued that the church must immerse itself in the betterment of society. However, although most liberals had undeniably good intentions, they so confused Kingdom and society that Christianity was reduced to little more than a form of optimistic humanism in which "A God without wrath, brought men without sin, into a kingdom without judgment, through the ministrations of a Christ without a cross".[121]

Such hopeful humanism lost all credibility in the blood bath of two world wars, leading theologians like Karl Barth to rediscover the evident sinfulness of humanity and the total "otherness" of God.

Sadly, however, many of those who reacted against liberalism swung to an equally unbalanced extreme. They so divorced Kingdom from society that the gospel became irrelevant to most things other than personal piety, and many wings of the church retreated into an isolated spiritual ghetto.

Even today, many pulpits resound with the theme that we must flee from society in order to be holy, which is the exact opposite of what Jesus did. As a direct result there are today second-rate Christian equivalents of most things that society has to offer from "Christian" music to "Christian" holidays and "Christian" dating agencies. I would suggest that this is an unbiblical way of interacting with society. That's why I don't claim to drive a "Christian" car, I drive a Volvo. I don't listen to "Christian" music, I listen to music and some of it is by Christians. We are called to live in society and to redeem culture, not replace it.

It is one of the disappointments of the Great Awakening that Whitefield urged his converts to "flee the world" and although he would readily call on the speaker of the House of Commons to stand up for the poor in Ireland or elsewhere, "he rated politics a distraction from heaven and best ignored by the godly. Thus the important people [sic] whom he touched were inclined to withdraw from mundane efforts".[122] He would pronounce that "There is only one real court, where Jesus reigns, and there he has erected a spiritual kingdom in the heart. All besides is tinsel and glitter." As a result of this sad lack in Whitefield's theology and despite his personal generosity towards the poor, the converts of this great revival hero surrendered the most remarkable opportunity to mould the course of British politics. It was only thanks to John Wesley and in the next generation William Wilberforce, that the Great Awakening had the social impact it did, as we shall see.

Justice and awakening

Bring me a God of mercy but devoid of justice and I will have no scruples in calling him a figment of your imagination

George MacLeod of the Hebridean awakening

The ancient Celtic church-planters that first evangelised the British Isles came closer than any to turning the heart of these islands to God.

Their approach was to establish monastic communities that served as hospital, school and arts centre, "a source not just of spiritual energy, but also of hospitality, learning and cultural enlightenment".[123] They thereby modelled a gospel that was holistic, addressing society's needs spiritually but also very practically.

Another inspiring example is the Great Awakening of the eighteenth century. Its tireless evangelist John Wesley has been described as both a preacher of the gospel and a prophet of social righteousness. He wrote, "The Gospel of Christ knows no religion but social; no holiness but social holiness".

The Great Awakening launched a massive justice movement, which substantially laid the foundations of the modern Welfare State. In a relatively condensed period of time newly energised Christians initiated the following services:

- Prison reform (John Howard)
- Job creation schemes (one Methodist meeting room in London was turned into a workshop for spinning cotton)
- The first lending bank for the poor was established in 1746
- The Sunday School Movement was set up in 1769 by Methodist Hannah Ball — this movement was the beginning of free education for all
- First Legal Aid schemes
- Housing provision and clothing distribution for the homeless.
- The abolition of slavery throughout the British Empire in 1833 (William Wilberforce spent much of his life fighting for this and it finally became law twenty-two days after his funeral)
- The colliery bill of 1842 abolished the slavery of women and children in British mines (Lord Shaftesbury)
- The important Lunacy Acts of 1845, compelling each county to make adequate provision for the mentally ill. (Shaftesbury again)

Fighting the slave-trade

Although the name of William Wilberforce will forever be associated with the abolition of slavery throughout the British Empire; there was in fact a whole succession of Christians working together towards this end. The Quaker mystic, George Fox, had taken a stand against slavery as early as 1657 on the basis of human equality before God. Enduring social opposition and even prison, his diaries read like the journal of some holy secret agent. In 1767 an evangelical, Grenville Sharp, won a legal battle to ensure that a slave should be freed whenever he set foot on English territory. A Christian student at Cambridge University, Thomas Clarkson, then wrote a prize-winning essay on slavery in 1785, and it was he that persuaded Wilberforce to take up the issue in Parliament. Just four days before his death, Wesley wrote to Wilberforce urging him to "go on, in the name of God, and in the power of his might, till even American slavery (the vilest that ever saw sun) shall vanish away before it."

In fact, the abolition of American slavery had to await another Awakening, for it was converts of Charles Finney's remarkable ministry that led the abolitionist campaign in America. Finney's revival bred a passion for social justice in "a handful of determined men, a holy band who pitted themselves against the social folkways of a whole nation in order to stand up for what their hearts told them were eternal, universal, 'higher' spiritual laws."[124]

The Salvation Army

Meanwhile, in Britain the awakening of the mid-nineteenth century was converting and commissioning social activists like Thomas Barnardo and William Booth. Booth (1829-1912) and his remarkable wife Catherine, launched the Salvation Army, which was probably the only Christian movement of the nineteenth century to effectively reach the masses. They took the gospel to the poorest communities, engaging in "almost every type of outreach and care for the poor and downtrodden imaginable."[125] Booth knew that there could be no distinction between evangelism and social action. In 1890 he wrote a book entitled *In darkest England and the way out*, setting out a blueprint for social reconstruction and the rehabilitation of an entire nation which was probably a century ahead of its time. A typical salvationist slum report reads: "Mrs W of Haggerston slum. Heavy drinker, wrecked home, husband a drunkard, place dirty and filthy, terribly poor, saved now over two years. Home A1, plenty of employment at cane-chair bottoming; husband now saved also".

One of the most dramatic episodes in the Salvation Army's great history involved one of William and Catherine's sons, Bramwell Booth and his young wife Florence. Florence worked in a Women's Refuge in London where she helped care for the casualties of prostitution. The scenario was horrific: it is estimated that there were eighty thousand prostitutes in London (and some of these were under ten years old).[126] Two thousand pimps worked Charing Cross alone. Customers were often powerful people, including M.P.s, and Queen Victoria's cousin spent "eighteen hundred pounds a year debauching English girls".[127] The age of consent in Victorian England was thirteen, (compared to twenty-one on the continent) and one M.P. wanted it lowered to ten.

Such realities were harrowing for Florence, but nothing could prepare her for the shock of what she soon discovered. She began to realise that there was an underground network operating which was capturing young girls and trafficking them as sex slaves. Masquerading as employment agencies they were shipping girls as young as eleven and twelve to rich paedophiles in this country or even abroad, drugged and nailed alive into coffins.

Bramwell watched his wife cry herself to sleep night after night and determined to expose this sex network, whatever the personal cost. Working with Rebecca Jarrett, a recently converted brothel owner and William T. Stead, editor of the *Pall Mall Gazette*, Bramwell hatched a remarkable plot. Posing as a wealthy abuser, Stead succeeded in buying a young girl from her mother for two pounds, using Jarrett as his go-between. They published the story in the *Gazette* and it "took the British public by storm in a way that can hardly be paralleled in newspaper history."[128] George Bernard Shaw, the famous author, offered to go and sell the papers himself wherever it was opposed.

Within seventeen days the Salvation Army had more than 343,000 signatures on their petition to Parliament, and within a month the House of Commons had raised the age of consent to sixteen. The underworld fought back and managed to get Stead and Jarrett imprisoned for abduction. But the Kingdom of Heaven had won the day thanks to the bravery of a young man who refused to ignore the plight of the oppressed.

Today, in a world that often tries to marginalise faith as socially irrelevant, and where Social Services have been hi-jacked by militant humanists, we should make ourselves familiar with the facts. Contemporary society's education system, Civil Rights Movement, Legal Aid and homeless provision, to name but a few, all have their modern roots not in humanistic philosophy nor in grand philanthropy but in the gospel of Christ and outpourings of his Spirit. "The Evangelical Revival made England aware of its social obligations... The revival encouraged a passion for social justice."[129]

Eventually the state picked up the tab for most of these services and the church, with a few worthy exceptions, abdicated responsibility for the poor. However that could be about to change. Western economies face crisis because with an ageing population they can no longer afford to foot the bill for social provision.[130] There is a drive, where possible, to privatise social care out to those who can make it most profitable. Somewhere along the road the number on the bus has changed, and the motivation that once was social justice has become capital gain. As a result there are increasing opportunities for the church to follow the lead of Jesus, once again, in creative and sacrificial ministry among the marginalised. The good news is that some great models are already in operation. Demos, one of the British Prime Minister's favourite research groups, recently reported that "much of the best innovation in the provision of local health, homelessness, community regeneration and drug-related services is now being shaped by people of strong religious beliefs."

Praxis makes perfect

The liberation theologians of Latin America argue that theology is something we must live out and not merely think about. They call this approach "praxis". Praxis says that it is not sufficient simply to diagnose a situation as unjust but that each one of us has a responsibility to take action against that injustice. This means that, for every person who reads and agrees with this chapter, the question is "What are *you* going to do about it?"

One liberationist, Gutierrez, says that it is not until Christians actively involve themselves with the poor that they will truly understand Scripture.[131] In the words of the former Anglican Bishop, David Sheppard, God has a "bias towards the poor". This is not to undermine the authority of God's Word, but to recognise it. After all, every one of us reads Scripture through the lens of our relative experience and so our starting point is important. For instance, a Buddhist, when reading that God is love, might understand love as a desire that should be quenched. And when he reads about the Kingdom of Heaven, he will assume that the Bible is referring to heaven as the end of conscious existence! He needs to change his starting point to truly understand God's word.

In the same way, when Christians in a Jewish or even Muslim culture read that the prodigal son worked with pigs, that fact will have an impact upon them easily missed altogether by Gentile Christians. Until we acknowledge our own cultural blind-spots, we will merely use Scripture to validate them, and until we take on God's priorities for the poor, by identifying with them in our daily lives, we may well fail to understand the drift of his Word.

Identification with the experiences of oppressed groups does have the potential to reveal whole new depths and dimensions in the Bible. To take an extreme example, if you are locked in a tiny prison cell, references to freedom and liberation will become profoundly meaningful in a way they could never be for those who enjoy civil liberty. If you are convicted of a crime that you did not commit, passages about God's justice and vengeance will take on new weight. If you are forcibly evicted from your land, the Promised Land becomes something you are praying for now as a reality in this life, and not just in the life beyond. If you are a slave, the plight of the people of Israel as they escaped Egypt and dreamed of a land flowing with milk and honey, may well become the paradigm by which you exist. If you are born into poverty amidst rumours of illegitimacy, rejected by your community, disowned by your closest friends, oppressed and falsely accused by the powerful; you may well have an empathy with Jesus' worldview that the secure and empowered will never be able to glean from books.

In the light of all that we have seen of God proximity to the poor, perhaps the liberationists are right and we should lend disproportionate weight to any theology done by the oppressed. But if the next great outpouring of God's power is indeed to be harnessed for the poor and the oppressed, it is critically important that we begin to address these issues now. We are called to prepare the way of the

Lord and it runs through inner-city tower blocks, immigration offices, prison cells, hospital wards and bed-sits. The joy of this calling is that in such places we will discover Jesus and be blessed ourselves. Those who sow small seeds of justice now may well transform the lives of thousands come the next great season of God's liberation. But what does this mean in practice?

Paul Boateng M.P. says that "to transform, we must first engage".[132] The gospel calls us to get practical, to dirty our hands by engaging at three different levels: personal, social and political.

Engaging personally

We all need to begin where Jesus did, by engaging with the down trodden at an interpersonal level. The Samaritan woman that he befriended at the well was severely oppressed. First she was a Samaritan, and Jews hated the Samaritans. Second she was a woman, and rabbinic teaching was that it was better to bury the Torah than endeavour to teach it to a woman. Third she was unpopular, the victim of social alienation within her own community. Because of all these things, Jesus went out of his way to show her love. But he didn't stride up to her flashing his credentials as Saviour of the Universe. He simply asked her for a drink, recognising that he needed her help. This is always where we must start. We do not engage with oppressed people as an act of charity, but because we "owe them a debt of justice".[133] An Australian aboriginal leader once said, "If you have come to help me, then you are wasting your time. But if you have come because your liberation is bound up with mine, then let us walk together."

In the middle of Jesus' busy schedule, at a time when he was hungry during the heat of the day, he took time out to prioritise someone that society counted out. Personal engagement is always inconvenient! Significantly it is this act of reconciliation and justice that provides the context for Jesus' famous observation that the fields are ripe and ready for harvest.

One of our youth leaders had a strong burden for the teenagers who hang around on a local housing estate. She began to pray for them, and would go, at least once a week, to spend time there too. The first time Vicky appeared on the scene these young people challenged her presence defiantly — they didn't want some religious youth worker hanging around in their space. They spat at her and insulted her, but she kept returning undaunted.

One day she was with them when a police car drove up. Two police officers walked over to the group and, not realising that Vicky was any different, said without any provocation at all "You lot are scum". As they walked away Vicky's blood began to boil at the injustice of the situation. Indignantly, she walked up to the men, explained that she was a local youth worker and added, in no uncertain terms, that she considered their comments inexcusable. At this, these two big men hurried away flustered.

In that single instant the groups' attitude to Vicky changed. By identifying with them and standing up for them, she had become one of them, and went on to have great conversations about Jesus. She had identified with an injustice and had been hurt by the words aimed at them and it unlocked something of God's authority and purpose.

We have to stand up for the oppressed in other ways too. For instance, there are times when Christians should resist the materialistic flow of our culture when it comes to what we buy or where we live. Some friends were looking for a big house and after much searching found the perfect one. But it was on a private road that would preclude many of those that Jesus would want to attract, and so they turned it down. John Wesley fixed his income at a certain level and for the rest of his life, in spite of considerable earnings, would give away everything beyond that sum. In contrast, so many Christians are in complete bondage to their mortgages, the financial burden of which is like a magnetic field draining everything else they do.

Engaging socially

It is a useful exercise to sit down and identify marginalised groups within your local community. There are often excellent projects in desperate need of voluntary help, yet sometimes Christians are so busy with church meetings or an internal agenda that they don't even know of such great opportunities for ministry. Some of my friends go along to a weekly sports club for young people with learning disabilities. Another friend builds relationships in our local deaf community. She is the only hearing person some of them really know, other than the professionals paid to work with them. As we do these very practical things, in very ordinary locations, we minister to Jesus.

Engaging politically

Prime Minister Tony Blair wrote that "Christianity is a very tough religion... It places a duty, an imperative upon us... to care about creating a better community to live in... It is judgmental. There is right and wrong. There is good and bad. We all know this, of course, but it has become fashionable to be uncomfortable about such language. But when we look at our world today and how much needs to be done, we shouldn't hesitate to make such judgments. And then follow them with determined action."[134] The rise of Hitler and Fascism in the 1930s presented German Christians with an enormous challenge. But many church-goers supported Nazism as a positive force for change which they felt sure would grow out of its racism. They admired Hitler's stance against pornography, prostitution and homosexuality. They also felt that their Christian duty was to submit to the state. With the advantage of hindsight it is easy to shake our heads disapprovingly, but are we really so different? Our predominant model of faith remains individualistic, far more concerned with issues of personal morality and middle-class family values than with broader issues of political and social concern. How neatly evangelical concern dovetails with the status quo and evades political controversy. We sit in cosy suburban living rooms with the Bible open upon our laps and the family gathered round. The Scriptures are applied diligently to everything within the walls of home: to family life, swearing and lying, television viewing, drinking, and thousands of private agendas. But we give so little thought to the implications of the gospel for the world beyond our front door.

Problems of injustice must ultimately be addressed at a macro as well as a micro level. How many times would the Good Samaritan have to find someone mugged on the Jericho road before determining to do something about the robbers as well as helping the victims? Ultimately we are compelled to address the causes of poverty, as well as treating the symptoms. But finding causes is always a complex challenge and requires reliable and up to date information regarding justice issues.[135] False accusations based on ill-informed emotionalism and conspiracy theories can ironically perpetuate an injustice themselves. However there are a number of great campaigns worth supporting ranging from Third World debt-cancellation lobbies to consumer boycotts. What are you going to do about this call to engage with injustice? Why not turn right now to the list of agencies in appendix two, contact one and ask for information?

While certain wings of the church have traditionally shied away from the bewildering world of politics, the gospel of justice obliges us to use our vote. What's more, there is an incontrovertible Christian duty to vote not for the best personal deal but unselfishly, for policies that will benefit first and foremost "the least, the last and the lost".[136]

The justice of Jesus is ultimately nothing to do with grand theory. It is about the integrity of individual people engaging with the world's poverty at a personal, social and political level as an act of worship for the one who was, and still is, despised and rejected.

[illegible]

[illegible]

[illegible]

CHAPTER 18

SIGNS OF THE TIMES

When evening comes you say, "It will be fair weather for the sky is red," and in the morning "Today it will be stormy, for the sky is red and overcast." You know how to interpret the appearance of the sky, but you cannot interpret the signs of the times.

Matthew 16:2-3

In the UK a few years ago March for Jesus took as its theme *The Battle for Britain*. On that memorable day, in towns and cities throughout the land many thousands of voices asked God a question: "If not us, then who? If not now, then when?" I believe God hears that heart-cry and has begun an extraordinary work in our time. Globally people are turning to Jesus faster than ever before.[137] We look with wonder at the church in China, where at least fifty million people have come to Christ in fifty years.[138] We shift our gaze to the vibrant and spectacular church growth in Africa where at least one third of the population has come to Christ this century.[139] And we can only worship God for the revival fires raging in Latin America. The Brazilian Geographical and Statistics Institute estimates that the evangelical community there is growing at twice the rate of the general population, and that by the year 2045 half of Brazil's total population could be evangelical Christians.

One Argentinean factory owner started to evangelise and has now seen over two million people respond to Christ.[140] Even in the hard, dark continent of Europe attitudes are shifting and change is in the air.

Who did not sense this change as the invisible walls of apartheid came crashing down in South Africa, or as crowds reduced the Berlin Wall to rubble? History shifts in these moments and eras collide. A German band, The Scorpions, caught this sense of history, of wide-eyed wonder, in their song *Wind of Change*:

The world is closing in and did you ever think
That we could be so close like brothers?
The future's in the air — can feel it everywhere
Blowing with the wind of change.
Take me to the magic of the moment
On a glory night
Where the children of tomorrow
Dream away in the wind of change.

I believe that the latter part of the twentieth century will go down in history as a time when the winds of the Holy Spirit blew with remarkable power. The Charismatic movement has spread in forty years across every denomination and geographical boundary. In 1985 Peter Wagner made a conservative estimate that there were 178 million Pentecostals and Charismatics worldwide, reflecting a decadal growth rate of 224 per cent. "If accurate, it represents what would undoubtedly be one of the highest recorded rates of growth of a non political, non-militaristic human movement across history."[141]

More recently God has stirred the church once more with a season of great refreshing: nicknamed by the mass media "Toronto Blessing". More than a million people have passed through the doors of one church in downtown Toronto in three years seeking spiritual renewal. In fact this heavenly waterfall attracted more tourism to Canada in one year than Niagara Falls! Significantly, such Holy Spirit phenomena occurred in Argentina for five years before the awakening.

In the UK attitudes are changing. In the wake of national tragedies there is a cry for morality and integrity. Politicians who, not so long ago, kept their lights under ridiculously large bushels are now considering Christian faith a distinct electoral advantage. The tragic death of Princess Diana shook the world and melted the traditional British reserve. Paul Johnson, writing in the *Daily Mail*, captured the moment well: "The surge of feeling for Diana this week has been a spontaneous, collective, religious act of the nation. It is a plea: 'Give us a spiritual dimension; make our lives meaningful; show us there is more to existence than getting and spending and acquiring'".[142] As the memory of Diana fades into the pages of history, the deep corporate longing which found momentary expression at the time of her death rumbles on.

The influential think-tank Demos recently advised the British Government that Christians would be an increasing force for change in the third millennium. It notes that while fourteen per cent of the UK attend church regularly, over half the population prays, believes in heaven and even the resurrection, concluding remarkably that there is an acute spiritual hunger in the land. Accordingly, over 100,000 people a year are attending the twelve-week Alpha course, investigating the claims of Scripture.

The media is picking up the theme. National newspapers are speaking in a matter of fact manner about "the spiritual re-birth of the nation" (*Daily Mail* December 1996). Even the hedonistic *Face* magazine humorously acknowledges that "After years in the popular wilderness, God is staging a comeback… reappraisal for the spiritual life is coming from the least likely quarters: scientific, secular and popular." (January 1997). It goes on to report that Stephen Hawking, supposedly the Einstein of our time, has renounced his previous atheism on scientific grounds. Even Mills & Boon, the publishing house behind thousands of fantasy romantic novels, is adapting to the new mood. Readers are apparently demanding less sex and more spiritually fulfilling story lines. Recognising the religious renaissance future novels will reflect important lessons about life, faith and love, aiming to promote Christian values whilst lifting the readers' spirit. Dame Barbara Cartland who has written more than six hundred titles told reporters: "I think it is good to reintroduce Christian values."[143]

Within certain communities in the UK there even appear to be pockets of revival. Chaplain David Powe and Gerald Coates estimate that 4,500 to 5,000 people have come to Christ in Britain's prisons since 1994. If correct, this amounts to one fifth of the entire prison population! Some fifteen thousand gypsies have also received Jesus in less than a decade. It is possible that such close-knit communities might serve as a barometer indicating a changing climate, or even as catalysts of change in the nation.

But...

But as we look at these remarkable signs of life, however, we should also remember that this century has known more Christian martyrs than the previous nineteen combined. All is not well in the western world with unparalleled materialism, depravity, social alienation and greed. Our scientists are relentlessly pushing back the frontiers of impossibility, while our moral boundaries collapse around us. We are becoming increasingly dangerous to ourselves and our planet; a people with more knowledge than sense. And ironically the younger generation's hope is no longer in Captain Kirk's optimistic vision of scientific conquest. Their faith is not in the untapped potential of tomorrow but rather in the past. Hope is increasingly retrospective, young people look wistfully backwards as they clothe themselves in nostalgic fashion and boldly go where pagan man has been before: to astrology and not astronomy, to ancient spiritualities and not futuristic fantasies. Admittedly they love the science fiction of Star Trek and Star Wars but only because its dated 60s and 70s chic reassures them of a past in which adults trusted the future like children. For this generation, science is the least plausible religion of all and they are hungry for spiritual experience.

But amidst this spiritual hunger the church is itself perceived as malnourished. The latest research suggests that Europe is becoming the darkest mission field on earth despite its spiritual heritage. In fact, if world wide church growth is to overtake the global birth rate, there will have to be an awakening in Europe which reverses church decline and releases the wealth of her resources to the developing world. And should such an awakening penetrate the Moslem communities of Europe it might well also be the vital key that unlocks the ten-forty window (the band of predominantly Islamic countries stretching from north Africa through the middle east to Asia).

It is an awesome responsibility to be entrusted with the gospel in days of such unprecedented opportunity and need. We have access to tools of mass communication unimagined by Wesley, Edwards and Finney in their wildest dreams. Billy Graham writes: "God has given us new tools to reach this generation. For centuries the preacher's audience was limited by the distance his voice could travel — a distance measured at best in tens of yards. Now that distance has become limitless".[144] Indeed these tools offer the most comprehensive potential for global evangelisation ever, if we will only seize the moment.

As we consider such potential, could it be that God is preparing us for an awakening that will propel the gospel to every corner of his world? Is it possible that the final rain clouds are gathering in our day? If the monsoon of awakening is indeed about to break, we must labour night and day to irrigate the land, to prepare ourselves, our churches and our communities for the King of Kings.

It was Lawrence of Arabia who wrote; "All men dream but not equally. Those who dream by night in the dusty recesses of their mind, wake in the day to find that it was vanity. But the dreamers of the day are dangerous men, for they may act out their dreams with open eyes, to make them possible."

Oh that God would once again raise up dreamers of the day: men and women who dare to live their prayers, a rebel force who despise mediocrity and subvert sin. Such a generation does not rest until it lays hold of that for which Christ died. It perseveres through the darkest night and the coldest winter to prepare for the impossible. Such a generation wrestles alone with angels, it knows its weakness and redefines success in its wake. Such generations hijack history, they rewrite the destiny of nations to the glory of God.

Let us prepare the highway of God through the wilderness of our hearts, our churches and our world, for the King will surely come. Revival has visited us before and it will come again. But what of us? What of our lives? Could God use me? Could he do it here? Could he start it now? Could we be the generation that finally carries the whole gospel to the whole earth that Christ may come again? Gracious God, let it be so.

> *Lord, I have heard of your fame.*
> *I stand in awe of your deeds, O Lord.*
> *Renew them in our day,*
> *In our time make them known;*
> *In wrath remember mercy.*

Habakkuk 3:2

APPENDIX 1

PHYSICAL MANIFESTATIONS ASSOCIATED WITH REVIVAL

I include this section because so many writers dismiss or ignore the physical manifestations associated with revival. I understand their reasoning because we do not want to be distracted by such phenomena and because there is a potential minefield involved in discerning that which is of God from that which is demonic or merely human. However we must also be careful not to dismiss aspects of God's power simply because they cause cultural offence. God delights in surprising us!

It should also be an encouragement to note that such manifestations have accompanied every awakening in every culture to some degree (even where it did not fit with the prevailing theology and was therefore suppressed and hushed up), and that the fruit of such power encounters is generally good. Revival is a sign that is spoken against for many reasons, and it would be tragic if well meaning people rejected a move of God's Spirit simply because of unusual manifestations, unaware that these are, if anything, a mark of authenticity!

However, I stress that it is the fruit of a power encounter that matters, not the sensational appearance. It has often been said that the issue is not what happens when a person falls down, but what happens when they get up. A mother of two who was not a Christian asked for prayer at one of our meetings and fell to the ground as the power of God touched her. As she lay there she silently gave her life to Christ and stood up as a new creation. But it is worth remembering too that, as far as we know, Jesus never fell, shook or laughed uncontrollably. Most revival leaders have worked hard to play down all such manifestations and a few have actively discouraged them. There is certainly never a justification for hyping crowds, since the manifestation is only ever as meaningful as the encounter with God that it expresses anyway.

The fact remains, however, that in this sophisticated age, physical manifestations appear to be an unnecessary stumbling block for many, and it is important to be clear that such peripherals accompany every move of God whether we like it or not. Whatever our disposition regarding physical manifestations — whether we are nervous or comfortable with such phenomena, we must never abandon the gift of discernment, since God likes to break our rules and challenge our preconceptions while the Enemy likes to distract us with counterfeits. If anything, we need to relax about unusual manifestations and take them less seriously, because they don't actually prove or disprove anything. As Jonathan Edwards says, "A work is not to be judged of by any effects on the bodies of men; such as tears, trembling, groans, loud outcries, agonies of body, or the failing of bodily strength. The influence persons are under is not to be judged one way or other by such effects on the body; and the reason is because the Scripture nowhere gives us any such rule."[145]

Please note that this list simply represents a few examples and is nothing like an exhaustive catalogue of manifestations.

Birth-pains

See chapter nine

Buildings shaking

George Fox (1642-91) in Mansfield: "After this I went again to Mansfield, where there was a great meeting of professors and people; here I was moved to pray; and the Lord's power was so great, that the house seemed to be shaken."[146]

In the village of Arnol, Isle of Lewis, Hebridean Awakening: "Around midnight Duncan turned to the local blacksmith: 'John, I feel the time has come for you to pray.' With his cap in his hand John rose to pray, and in the middle of his prayer he paused, raised his right hand to heaven, and said: 'O God, you made a promise to pour water upon him that is thirsty and floods upon the dry ground, and, Lord, it's not happening.' He paused again and then continued: 'Lord, I don't know how the others here stand in your presence; I don't know how the ministers stand, but, Lord, if I know anything about my own heart I stand before Thee as an empty vessel, thirsting for Thee and a manifestation of Thy power.' He halted again and after a moment of tense silence cried: 'O God, Your honour is at stake, and I now challenge You to fulfil Your covenant engagement and do what you have promised to do.' Many who were present witnessed that at that moment the house shook. Dishes rattled in the sideboard, as wave after wave of Divine power swept through the building."[147]

Crying out, weeping, groaning

Numerous examples. For instance, accompanying Wesley's preaching: "Cries and groans and quaking had sometimes accompanied the preaching. (Charles Wesley had noted at Blackheath in England that 'the cries of the wounded were heard on every side,' and when Wesley wrote his famous hymn, *Love divine, all loves excelling,* he meant literally the line *Enter every trembling heart.*)"[148]

Rev. Robert Murray McCheyne, Dundee revival: "I have myself frequently seen the preaching of the Word attended with such power, that the feelings of the people could not be restrained. I have heard individuals cry aloud as if pierced through with a dart... every sentence has been responded to by the bitterest agony. At such times I have seen persons so overcome that they could not walk or stand."[149]

Death

A number of Charles Finney's opponents dropped dead. In one case, Finney had been invited to preach in the church of an immoral pastor; "God struck down the infidel preacher and during the meeting he died a horrible death".[150]

Drunkenness

Howell Harris (1714-1773): "Sealed in the Spirit... 'til two in the morning like a drunken man, could say nothing but 'glory', 'glory' for a long time."[151]

Howell Harris speaking to Wesley after hearing him preach: "Before you were done, I was so overpowered with joy and love that I had much trouble walking home."[152]

Faces shining

Evan Roberts just prior to the Welsh awakening: "In the Sunday service

Roberts' friends noticed that his face was shining. In the youth prayer meeting, tears streamed from his eyes as he prayed repeatedly, 'Glorify Thy Son'."[153]

A new convert of the Hebridean Awakening: "Later, as he met an elder by the roadside, a circle of light seemed to envelop them and looking up to locate the source he found himself gazing into the face of his Saviour."[154]

Falling down

Edwards, New England Awakening: "...it is not at all strange that God should sometimes give his saints such foretastes of heaven, as to diminish their bodily strength."[155]

May 14th 1740, Nottingham, Delaware, USA: While George Whitefield was preaching to twelve thousand people, "Men and women dropped as dead, then revived, then fainted again, as George preached on, swept up into contemplation of 'Christ's all constraining, free and everlasting love' until, as he reached a last appeal to come to the cross... George himself fell in a swoon. For a few moments the Tennent brothers believed he was dead."[156]

March 14th 1859, County Antrim: "Presbyterian, Anglican, Methodist, and Roman Catholic were gripped by the Holy Spirit and stood as if paralysed... A number of people were so smitten down by the Holy Spirit that they lay prostrate on the ground. These prostrations occurred repeatedly thereafter throughout the revival."[157]

1859, Northern Ireland: A man "was walking along the road counting his money. Suddenly he was struck by such conviction that he fell on the ground, like Saul of Tarsus, and his money was scattered on the road... Roman Catholics sitting in their chapels during Mass were stricken down."[158]

Hearing heavenly music

Hebrides: "Suddenly the sky was filled with the sound of angelic voices singing. Everyone heard it and they fell to their knees in the field... Twice before during Campbell's ministry, God in his grace had caused the people to hear heavenly music. Once during the Lewis revival in the early morning hours, as a group was walking through a glen, the heavens seemed to be filled with angelic praise, until another minister present cried for joy: 'This is heaven! This is heaven!'"[159]

Jumping

Indian Awakening: "They jumped up and down for joy for hours without fatigue; in fact they were stronger for it."[160]

Nineteenth century Wales: The Christians gained the nickname "Welsh jumpers" according to the late Professor Tudor Jones.

Laughter

A solicitor's office in New Jersey, 1821; the contagious effect of Charles Finney's Spirit baptism: "The Holy Spirit descended upon me in a manner that seemed to go through me, body and soul. I could feel the impression, like a wave of electricity going through and through me... I wept aloud with joy and love. I literally bellowed out the unspeakable overflow of my heart... A member of my choir came into the office to see me... 'Mr Finney, what's wrong with you?' I could not answer for some time... He turned and left the office, and in a few minutes returned with one of the elders of the church... This elder was a very serious man and in my presence had been very watchful. I had scarcely ever seen him laugh. When he came in I was very much in the state in which I was when the young man went out to call him. He asked me how I was and I began to tell him. Instead of saying anything he fell into a most spasmodic laughter. It seemed as if it was impossible for him to keep from laughing from the very bottom of his heart."[161]

Assam revival, India 1905: "One little girl of twelve is constantly laughing... You think you have looked on an angel face. Some claim to have seen the Lord — one, a blind girl. All speak of his coming again."[162]

Memory recall

1859, Northern Ireland: "In some instances those prostrated while seemingly oblivious to all else showed wonderfully anointed memory. One pastor told of a girl with fixed eyes turned to heaven for four hours. She quoted over a hundred scriptures all related and applied to her own case. She repeated sermons and exhortations that the pastor had preached over previous months, quoting large sections of these verbatim. Afterwards the pastor questioned her, but she could not remember the sermons or quote those scripture passages accurately as she had done when gripped by the Holy Spirit."[163]

Mist or cloud

Azusa Street outpouring, Frank Bartleman: "A sister tried to persuade me to discontinue the prayer meetings I had started. I asked the Lord to show me his will in the matter. He came and filled our little cottage with a cloud of glory until I could scarcely bear his presence. That settled it for me."[164]

Shaking or trembling

This is how the Quakers got their name. George Fox recounts an amusing example: "Captain Drury… would scoff at trembling, and call us Quakers, as the Independents and Presbyterians had nick-named us before. But afterwards he once came to me and told me that as he was lying on his bed to rest himself in the day-time, a sudden trembling seized him, so that his joints knocked together, and his body shook so that he could not rise from his bed… But he felt the power of the Lord was upon him, and fell off his bed, and cried to the Lord, and said, he never would speak against the Quakers, or such as trembled at the word of God."[165]

John Wesley: "I shook from head to foot, while tears of joy ran down my face."[166]

Charles Finney: "The Lord drew so near to me that my flesh literally trembled on my bones. I shook from head to foot under the full sense of the presence of God."[167]

Trances

Stornaway, Hebridean Awakening: "A young woman in particular repeatedly went into trances, in which she received messages concerning those in need which she passed on to Duncan Campbell. One night he was staying in Stornaway when this girl saw a vision of a woman in agony of soul twenty miles away… and without any thought for his own rest or safety Duncan motorcycled to the village and found it exactly as he had been told… Not one word given by this girl through her trance-visions proved false."[168]

Mukti school, India: "About twenty girls went into a trance at one time and became unconscious of this world for hours; some for three or four days. During that time they sang, prayed, clapped their hands, rolled about, or sat still. When they became conscious they spoke of seeing a throne in heaven, a white robed throng and a glory so bright they could not bear it."[169]

Visions

Dazzling light, Welsh revival 1904, Anglesea: "The holy presence of God was so manifested that the speaker himself was overwhelmed; the pulpit where he stood was so filled with the light of God that he had to withdraw!"[170]

Visions of fire

Mukti school, India 1905: "The Spirit was pored out on one of the seeking girls in the night. Her companion sleeping next to her awoke, and seeing fire enveloping her, ran across the dormitory and brought a pail of water to dash upon her. In less than an hour, all the girls were weeping, praying and confessing their sins. Many of these girls were invested with a strange, beautiful and supernatural fire."[171]

Moving images projected on the walls

Kara Camp, India: "At Kara Camp pictures appeared on the walls to a company of small girls in prayer, supernaturally depicting the life of Christ. the figures moved in the pictures and were in colours. Each view would last from two to ten minutes and then the light would gradually fade away, to reappear in a few moments with a new scene. These appeared for twelve hours and were not only seen by the native children of the orphanage and eight missionaries, but by native Christians living nearby. Even heathens came to see the wonderful sight."[172]

Balls of fire

"In Wales, coloured lights were often seen, like balls of fire, during the revival."[173]

Finally, here is an account from the cricketer and famous missionary C.T. Studd during the 1914 revival in Belgian Congo which incorporates most of the manifestations listed above!

> *The whole place was charged as with an electric current. Men were falling, jumping, laughing, crying, singing, confessing, and some were shaking terribly. It was a terrible sight... This particular one can best be described as a spiritual tornado. People were literally flung to the floor or over the forms, yet no-one was hurt... As I led in prayer, the Spirit came down in mighty power, sweeping the congregation. My whole body literally trembled with power. We saw a marvellous sight, people literally filled and drunk with the Spirit.*[174]

While appreciating the fact that all such manifestations are common to revival, let us finish this section with a word of gentle caution from Professor Richard Lovelace writing in *Christianity Today* (November 11th 1995):

> *A revival movement that finds itself replicating compulsive laughter, spiritual drunkenness, pecking like chickens or roaring like lions as expected aspects of spiritual awakening may be playing into the Enemy's hands. It is in the Devil's interest to make Christians weird. He does not need possession to do this; he can manage by suggestion. The goal of his strategy is to create a church that is so institutionally strange that unbelievers will detour around it. The goal of revival is conformity to the image of Christ, not imitation of animals... Edwards' own final approach to the Great Awakening was to subject it to the most rigorous critique, on the one hand, and to solicit extraordinary prayer for its advancement, on the other. These are strategies we need to follow today.*

APPENDIX 2

Engaging with justice issues

Children's rights, street kids and child prostitution

Jubilee Action 01483 894787

Child labour

Anti Slavery International
0171 924 9555

Ethical shopping

Christian Aid 0171 620 4444
Cafod 0171 733 7900

Facts about the ethics of multinational corporations

World Development Movement
0171 737 6215

Human rights / prisoners of conscience

Amnesty International
0171 814 6200

Nestle Boycott

Baby Milk Action 01223 464 420

Homelessness

Shaftesbury National Housing Coalition 0181 239 5557
Shelter 0171 505 2000

Lifestyle issues — what you can do in your everyday life

Cred 01243 531898
www.cred.org.uk

Racism

Evangelical Christians for Racial Justice 0181 985 2764

Refugees / immigration

The Refugee Council
0171 820 3000

Third World relief and development work

Tear Fund 0181 977 9144
Also check out www.oneworld.org

ENDNOTES

Introduction

1 J.I. Packer, *New Dictionary of Theology*, ed. Ferguson & Wright; IVP; p.588

2 The Oxford Association for Research in Revival

3 Arthur Wallis, *In the Day of Thy Power*; C.L.C, 1956

Chapter 1

4 Tim Beougher & Lyle Dorsett (Ed.), *Tears of Revival*; Kingsway, 1995; p.103

5 Historical references to such shaking can be found in Appendix one.

6 Beougher & Dorsett, *Tears of Revival*; Kingsway 1995; p.103

7 Richard F. Lovelace, *Christianity Today*; 11th September 1995; p.28

8 John Stott, *The Message of Acts*; Eerdmans, 1990; p.61

9 Nicky Gumbel, *The Heart of Revival*; Kingsway, 1997; p.16

10 As far as I am aware, Roger Forster first popularised this helpful piece of alliteration

11 Duncan Campbell depicts revival as "a community saturated with God", and this is explored in chapter four.

Chapter 2

12 Bono and The Edge, *Pop*; Polygram International Music Publishing, 1997

13 Beougher & Dorsett, *Tears of Revival*; Kingsway, 1995. See Robert E. Coleman in Appendix 1, p.101

14 *Ethix*, November 1997

Chapter 3

15 Martin Scott, *Transforming Society*; a paper presented in June 1997

16 John White, *When the Spirit Comes with Power*; Hodder & Stoughton, 1992; p.48

17 Scott, *Transforming Society*

Chapter 4

18 Jonathan Edwards, *Journal of David Brainerd*

19 Wheaton Alumni, January–February 1943, cited Beougher & Dorsett, *Tears of Revival*; Kingsway, 1995.

20 See Arthur Wallis, *Day of Thy Power*; C.L.C, 1956; also Wesley Duewell, *Revival Fire*; Zondervan; pp. 133-134

21 Duncan Campbell, *The Lewis Revival*; Faith Mission Recordings, Gilmerton Road, Gilmerton, Edinburgh EH17 8QG

22 R.B. Jones, *Rent Heavens*; Stanley Martin & Co, Ltd, 1930; pp. 43-44

23 John Pollock, *John Wesley*; Lion, 1989; p.103

Chapter 5

24 Campbell, *Principles that Govern a Spiritual Quickening*; Faith Mission Recordings

25 Frank Bartleman, *Another Wave of Revival*; Whitaker House, 1982

26 This account is given in more detail in Duewell, *Revival Fire*; pp.44-48. Also see James Gilchrist Lawson, *Deeper Experiences of famous Christians*; The Warner Press, 1911; p.79

27 Nicky Gumbel, *The Heart of Revival*; Kingsway, 1997

Chapter 6

28 St John of the Cross (Halcyon Blackhouse Ed.), *The dark night of the soul*; Hodder & Stoughton, 1988; p.61

29 Jonathan Edwards, *Journal of David Brainerd*

30 Hugh Black, *Revival — Personal Encounters*; New Dawn, 1993; p.29

31 A. Skevington Wood, *The History of Christianity*; Lion Publishing, 1990; p.447

32 James Burns & Andrew W. Blackwood, Sr., *Revivals, their Laws & Leaders*; Baker, 1960; pp. 288-89

33 Dr. P.V. Jenness, paraphrase of an address on the eighteenth century revival: *The History of Christianity*; Lion, 1977

34 From a recording of Duncan Campbell, *The Lewis Revival*; The Faith Mission, Gilmerton Road, Gilmerton, Edinburgh EH17 8QG

Chapter 7

35 Arthur Wallis, *In the Day of Thy Power*; C.L.C, 1956

36 Duncan Campbell, *God's Hand Upon a Man*; Faith Mission Recordings

37 Charles G Finney, *Lectures on Revival*; Bethany House Publishing, 1988; p.22

38 Stephen Neill, *Christian Faith and other Faiths*; IVP, 1984; p.22

39 Palladius, *The Lausiac History*

40 Barclay, *Ethics in a Permissive Society*; Fount

Chapter 8

41 Duewell, *Revival Fire*; p.357

42 A recording of Duncan Campbell, *God's Hand Upon a Man*; The Faith Mission

43 The only apparent conflict with this stance on faith comes in passages (almost all in Matthew) where Jesus uses the phrase "You of little faith". In the light of the broader context I suggest that Jesus is not referring here to a quantity of faith, but is rather using a gentler turn of phrase to describe individuals who were simply unbelieving. When speaking corporately he was much more direct: "Unbelieving generation", but to individuals who were often sick and non-religious he spoke with great compassion. You can almost see him smiling sadly, looking them deep in the eyes, a slight shake of the head and a sigh — "Oh you of little faith".

44 Roger Steer, *J. Hudson Taylor — A Man in Christ*; OMF: 1990; p.298

45 Wallis, *In the day of Thy Power*; p.118

46 Charles G. Finney, *Lectures on Revival*; Bethany House, 1988; p.52

47 Everett Fullam in a sermon at Holy Trinity Brompton: *Heart of Revival*, pp.34-36

Chapter 9

48 Tom Sine, The Mustard Seed Conspiracy (Marc Europe), pp.1-5

49 Roger Steer, *J. Hudson Taylor — A Man in Christ*; OMF: 1990; p.25

50 Wallis, *Day of Thy Power*

51 Finney, *Lectures on Revival*; p.24

52 Finney, *Lectures on Revival*; p.58

53 Peter Wagner, *The Awesome Argentina Revival: Lessons in Evangelism & Spiritual Warfare from Argentina* http://www.christianword.org/revival/argentina.html

54 Finney, *Lectures on Revival*; 2

55 Hugh Black, *Revival — Personal Encounters*; New Dawn, 1993; p.77

56 Frank Bartleman, *Another Wave of Revival*; Whitaker House, 1982; p.23

Chapter 10

57 T.W. Manson, *The Illustrated Bible Dictionary*; Inter Varsity Press, 1980; Vol 2, p.1272.

58 See also Nehemiah Chapter 1 and John Dawson, *Taking Our Cities for God*; Word Books, 1989; Section 3

59 See Ed Silvoso, *That None Should Perish*; Regal Books, 1994

60 Hugh Black, *Revival — Personal Encounters*; New Dawn, 1993; p.116

Chapter 11

61 *Daily Telegraph*, 27th March 1996

62 John Hayward, *Mathematical Modelling of Church Growth* (Technical Report UG-M-95-3)

63 Though please note that today's mass media could undoubtedly accelerate public awareness of the beginnings of a national awakening in a particular location.

64 Alan Kreider, *Worship & Evangelism in Pre-Christendom*; Grove Books, 1995; pp.15-17

65 Richard F Lovelace, *Dynamics of Spiritual Life — an Evangelical Theology of Renewal*; Paternoster, 1979; p.168

Chapter 12

66 Elton Trueblood, *Your Other Vocation*; Harper & Brothers, 1952; p. 32: cited William A Beckham, *The Second Reformation*; Touch Publications, 1995

67 See British Parliamentary Papers: No. 2253, Shipping Casualties (Titanic) 1912

68 See Appendix One

69 David Watson, *One in the Spirit*

70 William A Beckham, *The Second Reformation*; Touch Publications, 1995

71 Minucius Felix, cited Alan Kreider, *Worship & Evangelism in Pre-Christendom*; Grove Books, 1995; p.19

72 William A Beckham, *The Second Reformation*; Touch Publications, 1995; p.43

73 From Luther's Works, Vol 53; p.63-64

74 Richard F Lovelace, *Dynamics of Spiritual Life — an Evangelical Theology of Renewal*; Paternoster, 1979; p.166

Chapter 13

75 Pete Greig
76 *English Church Census 1979-1989*; MARC Europe
77 Archbishop George Carey in an interview with Mike Pilavachi: The church, young people and the future; *Soul Survivor* magazine; February/March 1998
78 Arthur Wallis, *China Miracle*; p.86
79 Andrew A Woolsey, *Channel of Revival — a Biography of Duncan Campbell*; The Faith Mission, 1982
80 Peter Brierley (Ed), *UKCH Religious Trends 1998/99*; Paternoster Publishing. Source: British Social Attitudes Survey, SCPR. Young people refers here to under 35s. Survey implied belief in a personal God, though 25 per cent of believers preferred to define God as a Higher Power.
81 Pete Ward, *Youthwork and the mission of God*; SPCK, 1997; p.127
82 John Wesley, *Wesley's Works, vol 8*; Wesleyan-Methodist Book Room; p.251
83 Richard Ashcroft, *Bittersweet Symphony*, from the album *Urban Hymns*; Abkco Music Inc.
84 Billy Graham, *Just As I Am*; Harper Collins, 1997; p.565

Chapter 14

85 Floyd McClung, *Living on the Devil's Doorstep*; Word Books, 1988
86 David Hayes, *Exploring Inner Space*
87 Billy Graham, *Just As I Am*; Harper Collins, 1997, p.126
88 Roger Ellis & Chris Seaton, *New Celts*; Kingsway, 1998
89 Please note that the preaching of people like Wesley, Whitefield and Booth was certainly not considered conventional and had undoubted mass appeal.
90 Floyd McClung Jr. & Kalafi Moala, *Nine Worlds to Win*; Word, 1989; p.59
91 Peter Wagner, *The Awesome Argentina Revival: Lessons in Evangelism & Spiritual Warfare from Argentina* http://www.christianword.org/revival/argentina.html
92 Peter Wilkes' analysis of the reasons for the success of the Argentinean power evangelism. Cited Peter Wagner, *The Awesome Argentina Revival*
93 Smith & Garrard, *Revival Town*; from the album *King of Fools*;

Curious? Music UK, 1997

94 Frank Bartleman, *Another Wave of Revival*; Whitaker House, 1982; p.34

95 Tony Campolo, *You Can Make a Difference*; Word UK Ltd, 1985; pp.46-47

Chapter 15

96 Duncan Campbell quoted by Wallis, *Day of Thy Power*

97 Terry Virgo, *From Refreshing to Revival*; Kingsway, 1995; pp. 11-12

98 Charles G. Finney, *Lectures on Revival*; Bethany House, 1988; p. 14

99 Clark Pinnock, *The Openness of God*; Inter Varsity Press & Paternoster, 1994

100 Peter Wagner, *The Awesome Argentina Revival*

101 *The NIV Study Bible*; Hodder and Stoughton

Chapter 16

102 Gary North, *Christian Reconstruction — What it is, What is isn't*; p.51

103 The Fast Show; Series 2, Part 2; BBC World-Wide Ltd, 1997

104 Such social redemption is, it seems to me, an unavoidable consequence of any dramatic increase in the Christian to non-Christian ratio. However I am not necessarily arguing for a post-millennial golden era preceding Christ's return. Scripture makes clear that the end times will be a time of polarisation, in which the light will shine brighter whilst the darkness grows blacker (2 Timothy 3:1-5). It is also clear that large-scale awakening is always met with significant resistance and demonic opposition. During revival, in spite of social transformation there will also be terrible persecution and we would be unwise to pray for one without also preparing our hearts for the other.

105 Donald B. Kraybill, *The Upside-Down Kingdom*; Marshall Pickering, 1978; p.36

106 Walter Wink, *Engaging the Powers*; Fortress Press, 1992

107 Greg Valerio, *Jesus, Justice and Empowerment*: a paper available from Cred, PO Box 58, Chichester, PO19 2UD, UK.

108 Fusion, P.O. Box 58, Chichester, PO 19 2UD and UCCF, 38 De Montfort Street, Leicester, LE1 7GP are two such specialist student ministries.

Chapter 17

109 The Week, 7th February 1998

110 Henry Porter, *The Independent on Sunday*; February 1998

111 UNICEF 1991

112 Tony Benn MP, on BBC 'Question Time' March 1997

113 Patrick Johnstone, *Operation World*; OM Publishing, 1993

114 The Samaritans

115 Bill Bryson, *The Mail on Sunday*; September 1998

116 I appreciate that this parable probably refers to the way that the sheep and goats have treated either a) persecuted Jews or b) persecuted disciples. However the dividing line is still one of care for the dispossessed. Liberation theologies interpret this parable in terms of Christ incarnate in the oppressed, as do many other traditions.

117 Greg Valerio, *Jesus, Justice and Empowerment*: a paper available from Cred, PO Box 58, Chichester, PO19 2UD, UK.

118 Donald B. Kraybill, *The Upside-Down Kingdom*; Marshall Pickering, 1978; p.36

119 Julian, Ep. 22 cited Alan Kreider, *Worship & Evangelism in Pre-Christendom*; Grove Books, 1995; p.20

120 Dietrich Bonhoeffer, *The Cost of Discipleship*; SCM Press

121 H. Richard Niebuhr (1894-1962)

122 John Pollock, *George Whitefield and the Great Awakening*; Kingsway, 1972; p.232

123 Michael Mitton, *Restoring the Woven Cord*; Darton, Longman & Todd, 1995; pp.41-48

124 Gilbert Hobbe Barnes, *The Anti-Slavery Impulse*; p.XIX

125 Winkey Pratney, *Revival, its Principalities & Personalities*; Huntington House, 1994; p.209

126 Madge Unsworth, *Maiden Tribute*; pp.7-18

127 Richard Collier, *The General Next to God*; Collins; p.11

128 Madge Unsworth, *Maiden Tribute*, p.25

129 A. Skevington Wood, *The History of Christianity*; Lion Publishing, 1990; p.452

130 In the UK £38 billion of a total £100 billion welfare budget is now spent on senior citizens — a rise of one third 1980- 1990.

131 G Gutierrez, *A Theology of Liberation*; SCM, 1989 and *The Power of the Poor in History*; SCM, 1983

132 Christopher Bryant (Ed), *Reclaiming the Ground, Christianity and*

Socialism; Hodder and Stoughton/Spire; 1993; p.66.

133 Pope St. Gregory the Great, 600 AD, Pastoral Rule 3.22

134 Christopher Bryant (Ed), *Reclaiming the Ground*; p.12.

135 Readers are encouraged to contact one of the agencies listed in Appendix Two

136 Gerald Coates

Chapter 18

137 However please note that church growth is not yet outstripping population growth, due to the dullness of the European church — Peter Brierley, *World Churches Handbook*

138 Gerald Coates, *Christianity* magazine, January 1998. NB. Conservative estimates put the figure at between 50 and 75 million conversions in 20 years. The figure may even be as high as 100 million.

139 Winkey Pratney, *Revival, its Principalities & Personalities*; Huntington House, 1994; p.189

140 Ed Silvoso, *That None Should Perish*; Regal Books, 1994; p.36

141 Wimber & Springer, *Riding the Third Wave*

142 Paul Johnson, *Daily Mail*; Saturday 6th September 1997

143 *Compass* magazine; Spring 1998

144 Billy Graham, *Just As I Am*; Harper Collins, 1997; pp.641-642

Appendix one

145 *Jonathan Edwards on Revival: The Distinguishing Marks of a Work of the Spirit of God*; Banner of Truth, 1994; p.91

146 *The Journal of George Fox*; London, 1852; vol. 1, p.63

147 Andrew A. Woolsey, *Channel of Revival, a biography of Duncan Campbell*; Faith Mission; p.133

148 John Pollock, *George Whitefield and the Great Awakening*; Lion; p.148

149 *Church of Scotland Report Evidence of Revival*; 1840

150 Basil Miller, *Charles Finney*; Bethany House; p.67

151 Eifion Evans, *The Welsh Revival of 1904*; Evangelical Movement of Wales; p.67

152 John Wesley, *Journals*; 5th June 1747

153 Wesley Duewell, *Revival Fire*; Zondervan; p.187

154 Wesley Duewell, *Revival Fire*; Zondervan; p.310 — See also Hugh

Black, *Revival — Personal Encounters*; New Dawn Books; p.67

155 Jonathan Edwards, *Distinguishing Marks*; Banner of Truth; p.92

156 John Pollock, *George Whitefield and the Great Awakening*; Lion; p.149

157 Wesley Duewell, *Revival Fire*; Zondervan; p.138

158 Wesley Duewell, *Revival Fire*; Zondervan; p.154

159 Wesley Duewell, *Revival Fire*; Zondervan; p.312-316

160 Frank Bartleman, *Another Wave of Revival*; Whitaker House; p.34

161 Helen Wessel (Ed), *The Autobiography of Charles G. Finney*; Bethany; pp.21-22

162 Basil Miller, *Praying Hyde*; Zondervan, 1943; p.36

163 Wesley Duewell, *Revival Fire*; Zondervan; p.154

164 Frank Bartleman, *Another Wave of Revival*; Whitaker House; p.37

165 *The Journal of George Fox*; London, 1852; vol 1, pp.186-7

166 John Wesley, *Journals*; 29th July 1759

167 Basil Miller, *Charles Finney;* Bethany House; p.59

168 Andrew A. Woolsey, *Channel of Revival, a biography of Duncan Campbell*; Faith Mission; p.135

169 Frank Bartleman, *Another Wave of Revival*; Whitaker House; p.35

170 Jessie Penn-Lewis, *The Awakening in Wales*; Paternoster Press; p. 45

171 Frank Bartleman, *Another Wave of Revival*; Whitaker House; p.35

172 Frank Bartleman, *Another Wave of Revival*; Whitaker House; p.36

173 Frank Bartleman, *Another Wave of Revival*; Whitaker House; p.36

174 W.E.C., *This is That*; C.L.C., 1954; pp.12-15